THE ASTRONAUT'S GUIDE TO LEAVING THE PLANET

T0104157

BY TERRY VIRTS

ILLUSTRATED BY **ANDRÉS LOZANO**

Workman Publishing Company

Library of Congress Cataloging-in-Publication Data is available.

ISBN 978-1-5235-1456-4

Design by Lourdes Ubidia
Cover illustration by Andrés Lozano
Photo Credits: **NASA:** pages 3, 12, 13, 16, 21, 34, 56, 64, 68, 70, 71, 85, 90, 96, 105, 115, 117, 120, 126, 132, 137, 140, 143, 144, 149, 150. **Photos courtesy of Terry Virts:** pages 5, 30, 43, 162.

Workman books are available at special discounts when purchased in bulk for premiums and sales promotions as well as for fundraising or educational use. Special editions or book excerpts can also be created to specification. For details, please contact special.markets@hbgusa.com.

Workman Publishing Co., Inc.,
a subsidiary of Hachette Book Group, Inc.
1290 Avenue of the Americas
New York, NY 10104
workman.com

Distributed in Europe by Hachette Livre, 58 rue Jean Bleuzen, 92 178 Vanves Cedex, France.
Distributed in the United Kingdom by Hachette Book Group, UK, Carmelite House, 50 Victoria Embankment, London EC4Y 0DZ.

WORKMAN is a registered trademark of Workman Publishing Co., Inc.,
a subsidiary of Hachette Book Group, Inc.

Printed in China on responsibly sourced paper.
First printing March 2023

10 9 8 7 6 5 4 3 2 1

CONTENTS

"THE STARS DON'T LOOK BIGGER,
BUT THEY DO LOOK BRIGHTER."
—ASTRONAUT SALLY RIDE

SPACE,
ACCORDING TO
AN ASTRONAUT

The roar of the rocket engines was so intense. I thought I had experienced a lot as a test pilot and fighter pilot. I've flown more than forty different types of aircraft. But the roar of the rocket engines was incredible. It was 04:14 on the morning of February 8, 2010, and I knew that one of the most significant events of my life was about to occur. I was the pilot of the space shuttle *Endeavour*, and we were going into space.

The roar, vibration, acceleration, and the sheer violence of that moment—yes, violence—shocked me. I was just a regular guy, sitting in a 4.5-million-pound space shuttle that was about to leap off the launchpad, and anything could happen. The light from the rocket's fire reflected off a thin layer of clouds hovering 1,500 meters (5,000 feet) above us, casting a blinding bright light for many miles. That's when you hear the crowd start roaring— when those clouds light up. The countdown began . . . 10, 9, 8, 7, 6, 5, 4, 3, 2 . . .

"Roll program, Houston" and "*Endeavour*, go at throttle up" were the radio calls between mission control and our commander, George Zamka. Though I had heard those calls a million times in training, being smashed against my seat by the mounting g-force, overwhelmed by the roar of nearly 10,500 kilograms (23,000 pounds) per second of exploding fuel, and seeing the night turn to day all made this actual launch a more intense experience than I'd imagined when I was in the simulator back in Houston.

Endeavour shot upward at more than 800 kilometers per hour (500 miles per hour) toward those clouds. I winced

The space shuttle *Endeavour* on mission STS-126, approaching the International Space Station with its payload bay open.

as we punched through this bright wall in the sky, and in an instant the sky became black. Finally, above all the clouds, we were enveloped in darkness, rocketing away from Earth, gaining speed at a dizzying rate, and climbing into an orbit that would eventually bring us to the International Space Station (ISS). Those first few minutes of flight were so spectacular and far beyond anything I'd ever experienced. I was in space.

THE ROAD TO THE LAUNCHPAD

Before I tell you all about what it's like to go to space, let me tell you about how I got to that launchpad. At the age of seventeen, I left home for the US Air Force Academy, and after graduating at age twenty-one, I began my journey as a jet pilot. I first flew F-16s as an operational pilot in the United States, Korea, and Germany, and finally as a test pilot back in the United States, at Edwards Air Force Base in California. After being selected by NASA as a shuttle pilot, I flew on *Endeavour* in February 2010 for the

International Space Station's final assembly mission, STS-130. We installed the Tranquility Node 3 module as well as the Cupola, a seven-windowed observational module. A few years later, in November 2014, I launched on a Russian Soyuz rocket out of the Baikonur Cosmodrome in Kazakhstan, from the same launchpad used by Yuri Gagarin, the first human to reach space. After docking with the ISS, we became part of the Expedition 42 crew. A few months later, a new Soyuz arrived, replacing half of our crew, and I became commander of Expedition 43, until I returned to Earth in June 2015, 200 days after launch.

Terry at the controls for the space shuttle *Endeavour*.

The Astronaut's Guide to Leaving the Planet is a book about adventure, about exploration, about the unknown. When I was young, I read my first book about space, and I was hooked. I grew up with posters of airplanes and rockets on the walls of my bedroom. And though most people told me I would never actually get to be an astronaut, I did not listen to them. I did not tell myself no! I learned how to become a pilot and astronaut, and I was always curious and tried to learn as much as I could in school and on my own about many different subjects.

When I was finally selected to be an astronaut and had a chance to fly into space and look back on our planet, it was the most incredible feeling. I am one of a lucky few people who have had the honor of traveling to space—my childhood dream come true. And it only happened because I didn't listen to others who told me I could never be an astronaut.

So no matter what your dream is in life, always remember—don't tell yourself no!

Are you ready to get started?

HOW WE LEFT THE PLANET: EARLY SPACE TRAVEL

If you are reading this book, you are following in the footsteps of all of the people who were astronauts before you. Because when we were kids, we were all curious about exploration and space, too. We all had a spirit of adventure, even though each of us came from very different backgrounds. Some of us grew up to become pilots, some engineers, and others scientists or medical doctors. But our dreams all began when we were kids, reading books a lot like this one.

Humans have always dreamed about flying, but traveling into space finally became a reality in the twentieth century.

THE SPACE RACE

The first person in space was Yuri Gagarin. He was from the Soviet Union (which broke up into several nations in 1991, the largest one being Russia), and he went onto orbit on a Vostock 1 rocket on April 12, 1961.

Yuri Gagarin

We use "in orbit" to describe satellites, telescopes, and other objects in orbit that aren't crewed. For orbiters, capsules, space stations, and ships, we use "on orbit."

A few weeks after Yuri's flight, American Alan Shepard launched in a Mercury capsule on top of a Redstone rocket from Florida. Although Yuri Gagarin's mission did a complete orbit of Earth, Alan Shepard's mission did not go onto orbit—it just went up

Alan Shepard

80 km (about 111 mi) and came back to splash down in the Atlantic Ocean. The whole flight lasted only fifteen minutes. It wasn't until John Glenn launched on an Atlas rocket on February 20, 1962, that an American finally flew onto orbit.

These early missions were the beginning of the Space Race, a competition between the Soviet Union and the United States of America. After World War II, the rivalry between the United States and its allies, and the Soviet Union and its allies, turned into what was called the Cold War. It was a conflict without direct

John Glenn

fighting between these countries, and the Space Race became a key part of the Cold War.

The Soviet Union quickly took the lead with the first unmanned satellite, called Sputnik, on October 4, 1957. President Eisenhower created the National Aeronautics and Space Administration (NASA) to oversee US civilian space exploration programs in 1958. The Soviet Union sent the first satellite and human to space, and also did the first spacewalk, but the Americans set their sights on something much bigger: the Moon.

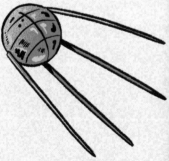

What were early astronauts worried about when they first flew into space?

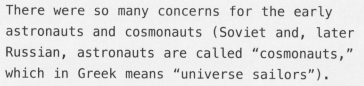

There were so many concerns for the early astronauts and cosmonauts (Soviet and, later Russian, astronauts are called "cosmonauts," which in Greek means "universe sailors").

Every phase of every early space mission was full of questions. Would the capsules maintain their air pressure? Would they be able to keep carbon dioxide levels from getting too high inside the capsule? Would the heat shields protect them from the fiery re-entry when they came back to Earth? The only way to find the answers to these questions was testing, trying, failing, and trying again.

Though every spaceflight is risky, those early astronauts and cosmonauts were true pioneers and very brave people. They still inspire me today.

TO THE MOON AND BACK

Shortly after Alan Shepard's fifteen-minute flight, on May 25, 1961, President John F. Kennedy told Congress, "I believe that this Nation should commit itself to achieving the goal, before this decade is out, of landing a man on the Moon and returning him safely to Earth." NASA quickly came up with a step-by-step plan to send people to the Moon before the end of 1969.

Photo of Earth taken by John Glenn, the first American to see Earth from orbit.

PROJECT MERCURY

Project Mercury was the first series of American spaceflights, and it showed that it was possible to fly into space. The first two Mercury astronauts were Alan Shepard and

Gus Grissom, and they each flew in a one-man capsule that did not make it to orbit. John Glenn became the first American to fly onto orbit on February 20, 1962.

THE GEMINI PROGRAM

Project Mercury was followed by the Gemini program, which tested new technologies we would need to go to the Moon. There were two big improvements in Gemini over Mercury—the capsule was bigger and held two astronauts, and its Titan II rocket was much more powerful than Mercury's Atlas rocket. Sixteen different

Ed White, the first American to walk in space during Gemini 4.

astronauts flew a total of ten manned Gemini missions in 1965 and 1966. These missions tested components that became vital to later space missions and gave rise to important American "firsts" in space, like rendezvous (maneuvering two spacecraft closely together) and docking (joining two spacecraft while on orbit), spacewalks, and long-duration missions of two weeks with two astronauts in the capsule.

THE APOLLO PROGRAM

Mercury and Gemini's success led to the Apollo program, which was designed to land people on the

Moon and, most importantly, return them safely to Earth.

The first Apollo mission had a terrible accident in 1967, a fire on the launchpad during training that killed all three astronauts. After that accident, NASA changed a lot of the procedures and equipment they used.

The early Apollo flights following Apollo 1 were for testing, and there were no astronauts onboard. Apollo 7 was the first mission that flew with a crew in space, and it flew to low Earth orbit (LEO) to test the capsule that would

hold the astronauts for launch and on orbit before parachuting back to Earth. The capsule was called the Command Module (CM), and it held three people.

Apollo missions 8, 9, and 10 continued to test key processes and components for the eventual lunar landing, including the Lunar Module (LM).

Finally, it was time to send Apollo 11 to the Moon. The three astronauts launched together in their giant Saturn V rocket. When they got to space, the CM separated from the rocket, turned around, and moved back in to dock with the LM, which was still attached to the upper stage of the Saturn V. The two vehicles then backed away

Apollo 7 CM.

Buzz Aldrin on the Moon, photographed by Neil Armstrong.

and continued to the Moon. Once they were on lunar orbit, Neil Armstrong and Buzz Aldrin got in the LM and descended to the Moon while their crewmate Mike Collins stayed on orbit around the Moon in the CM.

On July 20, 1969, Neil Armstrong became the first human to set foot on the Moon, just eight years after the first human being flew in space. He said one of the most famous lines of all time: "That's one small step for man, one giant leap for mankind."

The next day Neil and Buzz lifted off from the Moon, leaving the first stage of the LM on the surface along with some experiments and an American flag. They joined up with Mike Collins on orbit and flew back to Earth, splashing down in the Pacific Ocean three days later.

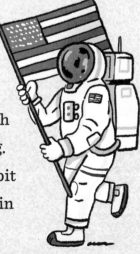

The Apollo missions that came after Apollo 11 saw astronauts land in precise locations on the Moon, collect scientific samples, and drive a Moon buggy—a small, electric-powered lunar rover that allowed for faster travel on the Moon's surface. Apollo 13 was the only mission that wasn't a successful Moon landing, but it demonstrated NASA's ability to safely return astronauts home following an emergency when their spacecraft experienced a large explosion in the oxygen tank.

The Apollo program taught us a lot about the Moon that we didn't know before we sent astronauts there, especially how the Moon and our solar system were formed. The Apollo 11 Moon landing is one of the most important events in human history, and people will always remember this amazing achievement. It is what motivated me to become an astronaut.

The last Apollo mission left the Moon in 1972, and nobody has been back since.

THE SPACE SHUTTLE MISSIONS

Our Moon missions were amazing and inspired the whole world. But they were also very expensive, and NASA wanted a spaceship that would be  cheaper than the large Saturn V rockets, which were not reusable. So they designed a reusable space shuttle that could carry seven astronauts and a large payload onto low Earth orbit.

The shuttle was used to deploy and repair satellites in Earth orbit, to launch deep-space probes like *Galileo* that eventually flew to Jupiter, launch space telescopes like Hubble, and conduct experiments in space. It was even used to help film several IMAX movies from orbit that have inspired millions of people back on Earth.

The biggest job the shuttle had was building and supporting the International Space Station.

What inspired you to be an astronaut?

When I was in high school, I read a book called *The Right Stuff* by Tom Wolfe. It was about Chuck Yeager, the first person to successfully fly faster than the speed of sound. Yeager trained astronauts for the early space program, and that book really inspired me and showed me the path to becoming an astronaut. After reading that book, I decided that I wanted to be a fighter pilot, then a test pilot, and then an astronaut. I admired all of the early astronauts, but Neil Armstrong was my favorite. He began as a Navy pilot and then flew for NACA (the National Advisory Committee for Aeronautics, the government agency that later became NASA) as a test pilot. He flew the X-15, an experimental rocket plane that flew at high altitude and up to five times the speed of sound! NASA used data from the X-15 program to help develop the space shuttle years later.

PARTS OF A SPACE SHUTTLE

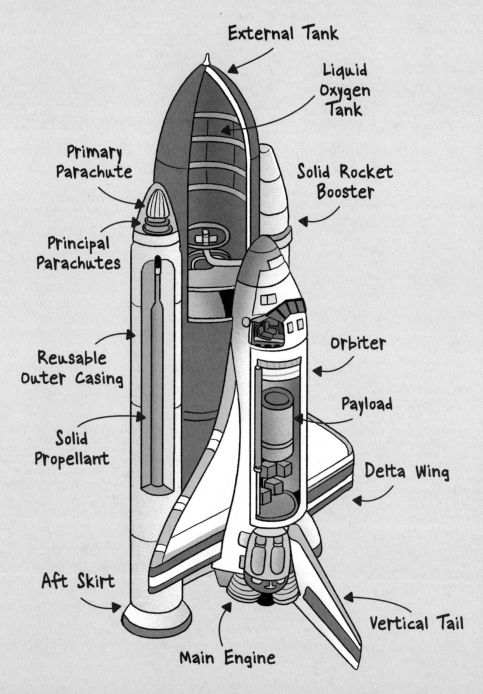

External Tank

Liquid Oxygen Tank

Primary Parachute

Solid Rocket Booster

Principal Parachutes

Reusable Outer Casing

Orbiter

Payload

Solid Propellant

Delta Wing

Aft Skirt

Vertical Tail

Main Engine

Three different shuttle orbiters (*Discovery, Atlantis, and Endeavour*) flew thirty-seven missions to the ISS between 1998 and 2011. They brought up new modules to add on piece by piece, like a giant Lego set in space. They also brought up astronauts and cosmonauts to be crewmembers on the station. And they brought up supplies like food and equipment used to keep the ISS running. The space shuttle was an amazing spaceship because it carried so much cargo, seven astronauts, a robotic arm, and the ability to do spacewalks. And it was reusable!

The International Space Station is a complicated spaceship, with lots of living modules and equipment.

THE JOURNEY TO LAUNCH: TRAINING

WHAT DOES IT TAKE TO BE AN ASTRONAUT?

Training for a spaceflight is one of the most fun things I've ever done in my life. In some ways, I enjoyed my time in training as much as I enjoyed actual spaceflight. One of the best parts of being an astronaut is doing different things every day.

During their training, astronauts take on many tasks, including conducting science experiments, repairing broken equipment, doing spacewalks, and packing or unpacking cargo ships. All of those tasks require a lot of training. There were things I had to learn that I'd never even considered before training began. One was learning how to be the crew doctor. This was some of my favorite training. I got to work in a local hospital and do things like give stitches and bandage burn wounds for people who had accidents in Houston. I even had a chance to work with a cadaver (a dead body) to learn how to give shots directly into a bone, in case a fellow

astronaut had a heart attack. If someone has a heart attack on Earth, and you have had CPR training, you can push on their chest to try to get their heart beating again. Well, in space if you push on their chest you'll go floating away, so I had to learn how to "stand" on the ceiling and push on someone's chest who was strapped down to the floor, using a dummy. It was also my job to control the medical supplies we had in space, so I had to learn what medicine to give, and when.

My favorite thing to do in space was making a movie during my last spaceflight! I was very excited when I had the chance to help film the IMAX movie *A Beautiful Planet*, because I had seen all of the space IMAX films since I was a kid, and I love cameras.

The director, Toni Myers, and director of photography, James Neihouse, taught me a lot about filmmaking, like the importance of lighting, focus, keeping the camera steady, and taking a mix of Earth shots and clips of the crew doing fun things inside the space station. I think making that film was the most important thing I did during my time at NASA, because millions of people have seen it and will continue to see it for years to come.

PREPARATION STARTS NOW

NASA teaches you much of what you need to know for space travel, but the truth is that astronauts spend their entire lives in training—your learning starts when you are a kid, and it continues, even as you fly in space.

There is no one simple thing that you can or should do in order to become an astronaut. NASA accepts all different types of candidates—pilots, doctors, engineers, scientists, military personnel, and even civilians like you are now.

All NASA astronauts have two things in common, though. Every one has a degree in science or math or engineering, and they're all at the top of their respective fields.

NASA pilots have been some of the military's top fighter and test pilots. NASA scientists and engineers are the top researchers at the forefront of scientific and technological advancement.

What were your favorite and least favorite subjects in school?

Ask an Astronaut

My favorite subjects were definitely math and science. Math was always easy for me, and I loved science. My favorite science was astronomy, followed by physics, chemistry, and biology. Another subject that I loved was French. I have always enjoyed learning other languages, and I really enjoy traveling.

The subject I did worst in was probably English. I was probably the least likely person in my high school to write a book, and now I'm an author. In fact, this is my fifth book! That has taught me that you can learn new skills that you never thought were possible.

Whether they end up flying planes or working on complex scientific research, all NASA astronauts begin at the same place: doing well in school.

Beyond the grades and the class rankings, astronauts need to be problem solvers, fixers, and good teammates. They need to be able to work under pressure, and more important than any technical or academic skill, astronauts need to be able to get along with other people. All the things you learn in kindergarten about being kind to others, cleaning up after yourself, waiting your turn, and working together as a team are vital to NASA astronauts.

Engineer and scientist applicants often have a private pilot license for light aircraft before they come to NASA. Other activities like scuba diving, mountain climbing, or even being a good car mechanic are very useful skills.

Math skills ✓
Good teammate ✓
Science experiment ✓
Problem-solving ✓
English ✓
Works well under pressure ✓
Physical training ✓

Another useful astronaut skill you can start pursuing right now is learning a new language. While US astronauts communicate with mission control in Houston, Texas, that's not the only control center for human space missions. There are also control centers in Moscow, Russia; near Munich, Germany; and in Tsukuba, Japan. There are also several smaller control centers in Canada and Europe that are used when required. I think the main reason NASA selected me to be an astronaut was because I spoke French and had lived overseas for years in Europe, Asia, and the Middle East.

Because every person is different, there are some parts of astronaut training that you'll be good at and others that you'll have trouble with.

Some astronauts struggle to fly jets because they weren't pilots before they came to NASA. Other astronauts struggle to do spacewalks. Even though everyone was at the top of their field before they got to NASA, each new astronaut finds something that is difficult for them, and the same will be true for you, too. Being challenged like this is one of the things that makes the job so much fun!

ASTRONAUT ACTIVITY

Imagine landing on the Moon or a planet like Mars and meeting another person or being. How would you introduce yourself? You'd probably say something like, "Hello, my name is Terry, and I am from planet Earth."

Here is how you'd say that in the following languages:

Ukrainian: "Привіт, мене звати Террі, я з планети Земля"

French: "Bonjour, je m'appelle Terry, et je viens de la Terre."

Chinese: "您好！我的名字是泰利，我来自地球。"

Spanish: "Hola, mi nombre es Terry y soy del planeta Tierra."

Hindi: "नमस्ते, मेरा नाम टेरी है, और मैं पृथ्वी ग्रह से हूँ"

Japanese: "こんにちは。わたしのなまえはテリー。ちきゅう から きました。"

Korean: "안녕하세요? 제 이름은 테리입니다, 저는 지구에서 왔어요."

German: "Guten tag. Mein Name ist Terry, und ich bin von der Erde."

Russian: "Привет, меня завут Терри Вёртс, и я из землей."

There are approximately 6,500 languages spoken around the world today. This is only a small sample to get you started.

ASTRONAUT TRAINING

When I was ready to begin my official training, I went to the NASA Johnson Space Center in Houston, Texas.

You're called an ASCAN when you enter training. This stands for AStronaut CANdidate. The initial training takes about a year and a half, and includes things like learning how to fly a supersonic T-38 jet, wilderness survival training, studying how the ISS works, learning how to

Flying the supersonic T-38 is the best training astronauts receive to prepare for spaceflight.

How much money do astronauts make and what kind of car do you drive?

Astronauts are employees of the US government, which means they earn a standard government salary. Some astronauts are in the military, like I was, so their pay depends on their rank. For both civilian and military astronauts, the lowest pay is about $90,000 per year and the highest level is around $170,000.

When I was first at NASA, I drove a Plymouth Laser, which was a fun car that I had as a fighter pilot. Then I bought a BMW Z3, a car I had always wanted. After having kids, I had to get a Ford Expedition to haul them around with all of their sports equipment. Then I eventually got a Honda Accord just to take me to the office and back.

I made a good salary and drove different types of cars over the course of my career. But have you ever looked out the window of a space shuttle to see the Sun rise over Earth? You can't put a price on that.

do spacewalks, studying the Russian language, physical training, and so much more. I know it sounds like a lot, but these are the basic introduction classes that will help you learn to be an astronaut.

After your basic training, you wait. And wait. And while you wait, you do ground jobs that support the astronauts in space. During this waiting period, I was a CAPCOM (Capsule Communicator), the person in mission control who talks on the radio to the astronauts in space. I also helped run our T-38 flying program, I supported a space station astronaut during his six-month mission in space, I was in charge of our robotics branch, and I worked with the SLS rocket program. I waited about seven years before I was assigned to my first space shuttle mission.

Training for my shuttle mission took a year, but training for my space station mission took more than two years. The International Space Station is one of the most amazing things that people have ever built. It took several decades, many billions of dollars, and more than fifteen nations to build this massive spaceship on orbit around Earth. It was built piece by piece, and each module was launched by either a Russian rocket or the US space shuttle. Most astronauts and cosmonauts spend about a half year on the ISS during their missions, where they do scientific and medical experiments. Science is the mission of the ISS. During my 200-day mission, we ran more than 250 experiments, from every kind of science—biology, chemistry, physics, astronomy, medicine, engineering, psychology, materials science, combustion science, you name it.

I spent more than seven months there on my two space missions, and my favorite thing to do was take pictures.

After I was assigned to both of my missions, I did a lot more of the same training. I had to learn how to fly the spaceships, how to fix things, how to do experiments, how to handle emergencies, some basic medical skills, study more Russian, and get into good physical condition.

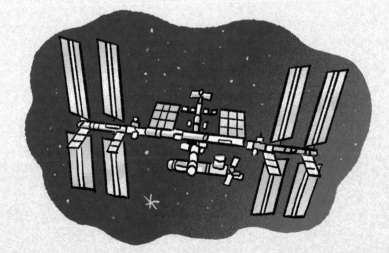

Why do you use a giant pool for training?

Ask an Astronaut

One of the world's largest indoor pools is at the Johnson Space Center in Houston, Texas. It is called the NBL, or Neutral Buoyancy Laboratory. It is so big that it holds more than 23 million liters (more than 6 million gallons) of water, weighing as much as 100 train locomotives! It is 60 m (roughly 197 ft) wide, 30 m (98 ft) long, and 12 m (39 ft) deep. There is a mockup of the space station in the pool, but the ISS is so big that only half of it can fit in the NBL. And even that has to be broken up into smaller pieces and rearranged so that they fit, like a Lego model.

Astronauts train for spacewalks underwater in NASA's NBL pool.

There is also a small amount of room for other things to be tested, like the new Orion capsule.

During NASA's Gemini program in the 1960s, astronauts began to do spacewalks for the first time, and they realized that it was very difficult to move around in weightlessness in a bulky spacesuit. They needed a better way to train. Buzz Aldrin was an avid scuba diver, and he had the idea that astronauts could use a special pool to float underwater and get used to how they would move around when they left their capsule and went out into space. So NASA built a series of pools where astronauts could practice spacewalking, of which the NBL is the newest and biggest.

There are some important differences between the NBL and real space. The first is that even though you are floating in water, you aren't weightless. Gravity still makes you hang down in your spacesuit. My arms and chest hung on the suit's metal rings, and I always had bruises after every six-hour training run in the NBL. The other big difference is the water. In the NBL it's very difficult to move, because you have to push yourself through hundreds of kilograms of water. If you stop pushing, you stop moving almost immediately. In space it's the opposite: A little push and you start moving, and it's hard to stop.

BODY BY SPACE

Physical fitness is an important part of training to be an astronaut—both on Earth and while you're in space. In space, your bones and muscles don't have to constantly work against gravity like they do here on Earth. That leads to atrophy, which means that they begin to decrease from not being used. You may be lying on the couch as you read this, and as you do you are getting a workout simply by holding up your head and arms. That 24/7 effort doesn't exist on orbit, and it has serious consequences. During the Russian Mir space station program in the 1980s and '90s, researchers learned that cosmonauts' bones would atrophy about 1.5 percent per month, no matter how long they were in space. It was as if they were on a straight-line

trajectory to becoming jellyfish. In addition to losing bone density, the space travelers also lost muscle mass, especially in the lower body, which led to serious problems upon return to our planet. Beyond basic bone and muscle health, there is another important reason to get and stay in shape: spacewalking. Putting on that beast of a spacesuit and moving around in it for eight to nine hours at a time is a serious workout, using a significant amount of upper body strength, endurance, and hand strength. That strength doesn't just happen on its own.

Every astronaut is different. There are thirty-year-old marathoners and mountain climbers and sixty-year-old "experienced" astronauts. The average age of crewmembers flying in space is probably around fifty. But space doesn't care how old you are or what your gender is. It also doesn't care whether you have time to work out or not. It only matters if you can do the job or not, and spacewalking requires you to be strong. Which is why astronauts make a real effort to get in shape before launch and stay in shape once in space. And then to rehab once they're back on Earth, too.

One of the benefits of being an astronaut is having access to an amazing gym. When I first showed up at the Johnson Space Center, the gym was a decaying relic from the 1960s. But then NASA built a new astronaut gym that would make any professional sports team jealous. It is roughly the size of a grocery store. The most interesting machine there is called the zero-g treadmill, in which you wrap a giant bubble skirt around your waist and inflate it with air. This lifts you off the treadmill while running, which means less leg impact, making it possible to run with less wear and tear on your joints.

We worked with an ASCR (prounounced "ace-er," which is the NASA acronym for personal trainer) for a personalized workout, as well as motivation to keep going. There was always a WOD (workout of the day) posted on the gym bulletin board that was a quick and intense body-weight program: push-ups, pull-ups, lunges, sprints, stretches, etc. There were also plenty of aerobic opportunities, with miles of outdoor running trails, indoor machines, and a pool.

In addition to daily exercise, astronauts are evaluated with an annual fitness assessment. It includes everything from a 1.5-mi (2.4-km) timed run or 800-m (875-yd) swim to max-effort bench and leg presses, push-ups, pull-ups, crunches, hand-strength and flexibility measurements, and everyone's favorite—a shuttle run around a series of pylons.

ASTRONAUT ACTIVITY

Going to space is such a physical test of the human body that astronauts have to do a lot of physical training before, during, and after a mission. Here is one physical activity for you to try, but please talk to an adult before you begin.

1. On your calendar, pick a week when you can practice this exercise every day. Find a path in your neighborhood, around your school, or at a nature reserve close by. Ask a parent or adult to help you figure out a 1-mi (1.6-km) route and go with you on your daily exercise—but be careful, and don't walk alone. Walk that route every day for a week and keep track of your time. At the end of the week, see if your time has improved.

2. Continue this for as long as you want, and keep checking your time. Walking is an excellent physical activity for the whole body. It will make your lungs strong and keep your heart healthy while also managing stress or anxiety.

AIR TRAINING

I love adventure, especially when it comes to flying. As a kid, my dream was always to fly. I would have been happy to fly a small Cessna 172 propeller airplane, so when I went to pilot training in the Air Force and got to fly jets I was super excited. I loved being in charge of an airplane as the pilot in command. And I loved flying fast and low and doing hard turns and "pulling g's," which happens when a fast jet turns, smashing the pilot down into their seat due to centrifugal force. Imagine holding a bucket full of water with one hand and spinning yourself around really fast until the bucket was flying along straight out from your body. Even though the bucket is up on its side, the water doesn't fall out because it is smashed to the bottom of the bucket by centrifugal force. The same thing happens to airplanes (or rockets) that are moving very fast when they try to turn—their crew is smashed down.

NASA astronauts fly the T-38 Talon jet as part of their training. It's an advanced supersonic jet trainer. The T-38

How often do you fly in space?

I was an astronaut for sixteen years, but I only flew in space twice. When I began my career at NASA, there were too many astronauts for the number of upcoming missions. Then there were several technical problems with the space shuttle that caused a lot of delays to the spaceflight schedule.

It took me almost ten years to fly my first spaceflight. Today, most new astronauts wait about five years to get assigned to their first flight, and then they fly a new mission every five years or so. A typical astronaut will fly a six-month flight two or three times in their career. I can say one thing for sure—flying in space was awesome and it was definitely worth the wait!

can fly faster than
the speed of sound, and
it can roll really fast because its
wings are so short and stubby. We
usually fly at more than 805 kmh (500 mph),
and sometimes more than 966 kmh (600 mph)!

Flying T-38 jets is the most important training astronauts get because it's one of the only "operational" things that we do. That means it teaches us how to think quickly during intense situations and how to interact with other crewmates when we have to make split-second decisions.

IN CASE OF EMERGENCY

Astronauts have to be ready to handle anything that comes their way, so emergency training is very important. We have to know what to do when something goes wrong, and we need to be able to stay calm.

The first thing that every astronaut has to do when they are learning a new spaceship is to study its different systems and understand how it's *supposed* to work: How it flies normally, how it controls itself, how it gets power, how the engines work, how it keeps the air inside the right temperature and maintains oxygen and carbon dioxide levels, etc. After you learn how things are supposed to work, you need to learn what to do when they break. One of the most important lessons I learned is that you shouldn't act too quickly when you see a warning light or hear the emergency tone. It's always best to wait a few moments and make sure there really is a problem—and then discuss what action to take—before you start pushing buttons. We had a joke that there was no emergency in the space shuttle that the pilot couldn't make worse with one switch throw.

Commander George Zamka and Terry at *Endeavour's* controls.

Of all the things I did as an astronaut, training for emergencies was one of my favorites. It was exciting and challenging and forced me to be at the top of my game. Learning how to handle space shuttle emergencies during launch and landing was very important for me because

ASTRONAUT ACTIVITY

Astronauts must be able to fix things if something goes wrong in flight, and they usually have to do it under pressure. Find an old toy or appliance around the house that you don't use anymore. Be sure it's unplugged and remove any batteries or power sources. With a parent's permission, use your tools (or ask to borrow some from a grown-up or even from your school) to take it apart and take a look at what's inside. Can you see how it works? Now find a stop watch and when you're ready, hit start and see how long it takes you to put the item back together. It's okay if it takes you some time! You can practice on this item or others to see if your time improves.

I was a pilot. I did hundreds of practice emergency simulations. As the shuttle pilot, I was responsible for making sure the rocket engines, electrical system, rocket fuel, and hydraulic systems were all working properly. Before I came to NASA, I thought this would be easy. Boy was I wrong! The space shuttle is by far the most complicated flying vehicle that I've ever flown, and I've flown more than forty different kinds of airplanes. It took me years before I was really good at handling every emergency situation that my NASA trainers could throw at me during our simulations.

ZERO-G TRAINING

The tradition of zero-g flights goes back to the beginning of the space program, when NASA wanted to find a way to give astronauts a taste of what weightlessness would feel like before they got to space.

The "Vomit Comet" is a passenger jet that flies in 161-km-long (100-mi) restricted airspace over the Gulf of Mexico. That means there is plenty of airspace in which to maneuver, and only certain airplanes can fly

there. The jet begins its maneuver at 6,000 m (20,000 ft) and noses over, accelerating to more than 640 kmh (400 mph). Then the pilot pulls back on the yoke (the steering equipment in an aircraft), smashing all of the passengers down on the floor at 2 g's, or twice their normal body weight. When the nose gets up to 45 degrees above the horizon, he pushes forward on the yoke until the plane is at zero g's, and the jet starts falling down toward the ocean below. This is a bit like being at the top of a roller coaster as it pauses at the peak of the tracks, except it's way more dramatic and lasts a lot longer. Once the nose gets about 30 degrees below the horizon, the pilot pulls back on the yoke, smashing all of the passengers on the floor, and then does the whole thing over again. After ten of these maneuvers, the Vomit Comit turns around and does the whole process again, flying in the opposite direction.

You have a similar feeling on a real space mission, because as soon as the rocket engines shut down after launch, you are floating, and that feeling doesn't stop until you come back to Earth, often months later. The reason weightlessness feels like you are falling is because you *are* falling! Even though the ISS is very high up (400 km, nearly 250 mi above the ground), there is still a lot of gravity from Earth. Because there is no ground to support the spaceship, it falls toward the center of Earth. At the same time, it is moving forward so fast (about 8 km or 5 mi per second!) that it never hits the ground. It just keeps moving forward and falling, and because its speed is exactly perfect, the shape of that motion is an orbit that keeps the ISS at about the same height above the ground for the whole orbit.

It takes a couple of days after you get to space to get used to moving around while you are weightless. One problem everyone has is when they try to throw something to a crewmate.

On Earth, we have to compensate for gravity and aim high when throwing things at a target. But in space everything is falling at the same rate and you don't have to compensate for gravity, so new astronauts are always throwing things too high. It takes a lot of concentration to stop doing that! Also, when you push off to float from one place to another, you not only move to the next place, but you rotate along the way. My first time in space, every time I pushed off to float to a new location I rotated and spun around so I landed in the new place pointed in the wrong direction. It took me a few weeks of practice before I was really good at floating, able to move from one place to the next while keeping control of my body and the things I was carrying. Being in a constant state of falling is a very strange feeling, but I loved it! It felt like I was Superman.

TRAINING STARTS NOW

There are some things you can do to train to be an astronaut right now. The activities throughout the book can help you prepare, and here are even more ideas to get you started:

1 Experiment! Be curious and investigate the world around you.

2 Learn everything you can in school.

3 Be a good friend and teammate.

4 Be a problem solver and learn from your mistakes.

5 Explore the natural world.

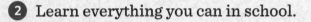

ASTRONAUT ACTIVITY

Experiencing weightlessness on Earth is hard because of gravity. But if you want to see if you can feel it for a single second, find a swing at a park, at school, or in your backyard. (Please ask a parent or adult to supervise you, and follow all of the rules at the location.) Pump your legs and swing—can you feel the second of free fall before the swing sweeps toward the ground?

BLAST OFF!: LAUNCH

There is nothing better than watching a rocket launch . . .

. . . except for actually being inside the rocket that is launching!

The noise, the vibration, the fire, the acceleration— launching into space is probably the coolest thing that humans have ever done. The first sensation I had during my space shuttle launch was hearing the engines fire up. The space shuttle had three main engines that used liquid fuel and two giant white rockets (which used solid fuel) that were strapped to the side of the massive fuel tank. Six seconds before liftoff, the three main rocket engines turned on, and *Endeavour*'s computers verified that they were running properly before we launched. At the moment of liftoff (what we call T-0), when the giant solid rocket motors lit, it got REALLY loud inside. Those two solid rocket motors dropped off the shuttle about two minutes after launch and parachuted back to the ocean.

My first launch was in the middle of the night, and it was pitch-black outside. But as soon as the rocket engines turned on, the fire from the exhaust lit up some low-level clouds. They were so bright that nighttime turned into

daytime, if only for a few seconds. As we lifted off and flew into those clouds, they got very bright and once we were through them everything turned dark again.

Because we were so tightly strapped in, we couldn't really look around that much, but I was lucky because I was the pilot and I could look out of my windows. I saw the East Coast of the United States at nighttime from hundreds of thousands of feet up, with all of its city lights. I could see the Moon out in front of us; it looked like we were launching to go there. And then as we flew over the North Atlantic, I could see the most beautiful, blue sunrise ever. It was a shade of blue I'd never seen before.

After the engines shut down, we were weightless. Some leftover oxygen and hydrogen rocket fuel turned into ice in the coldness of space, and it floated up past my window. The Sun was shining on these bright ice particles, and it was a show of sparkling ice unlike anything I had ever seen.

WHAT IS "SPACE"?

It seems like space is very far away, but it is closer than you think. The traditional definition of outer space is everything above the Kármán line, which is 100 km (62 mi) above Earth. (The Air Force awards its pilots astronaut wings if they fly above 80 km, or 50 mi, which is a little lower than the Kármán line.) Why is 100 km (62 mi) the magic number for the altitude of space? Theodore von Kármán, a Hungarian American scientist, is the person who calculated this. As airplanes fly higher and higher the air gets thinner, and because of that thin air, they have to fly faster so that their

Theodore von Kármán

wings can generate enough lift to hold them up. If an airplane is flying at an altitude of 100 km (62 mi), the air is so thin that it doesn't have enough lift to support it and it would be flying so fast that it's on orbit. So, if you are flying above 100 km (62 mi), you are considered to be in space, and below this altitude you are considered to be flying in the atmosphere. That's how Mr. von Kármán came up with the definition of space.

How long does it take to get to space?

Ask an Astronaut

It took the space shuttle a little more than four minutes to climb above 100 km (62 mi) in altitude, and by that point it was traveling at more than 2 km (1.2 mi) EVERY SECOND! The shuttle's main rocket engines kept running for about eight and a half minutes until it was finally on orbit, floating weightlessly, and flying almost 8 km (5 mi) per second! To understand how fast that is, a car speeding on a highway takes more than a minute to go 2 km. Rockets travel about 300 times faster than cars!

PARTS OF A SPACESUIT

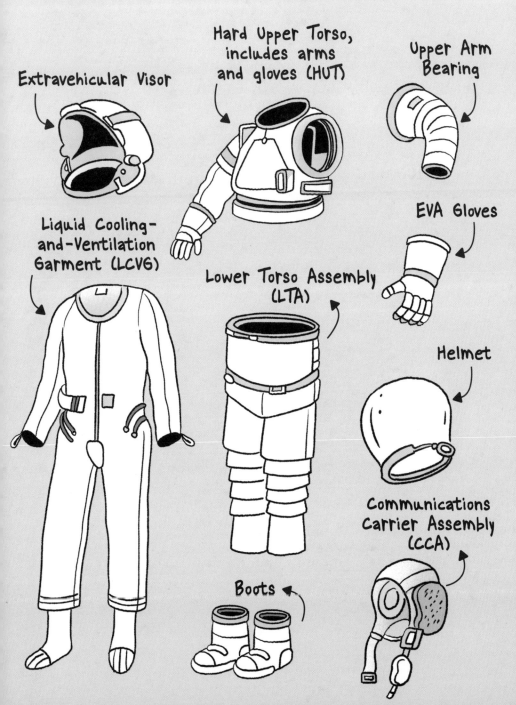

Extravehicular Visor

Hard Upper Torso, includes arms and gloves (HUT)

Upper Arm Bearing

EVA Gloves

Liquid Cooling-and-Ventilation Garment (LCVG)

Lower Torso Assembly (LTA)

Helmet

Communications Carrier Assembly (CCA)

Boots

PREPARING FOR LIFTOFF

Getting ready for launch takes a long time. A launch spacesuit is really difficult to put on. It takes a team of a few technicians almost an hour to help you get into your suit. You put the space shuttle spacesuit (called ACES) on in several parts.

The first step was a base layer that was like long underwear. Next was a cooling garment that has water tubes in it to help cool you down. Then came the actual spacesuit, which had a rubber layer to hold air pressure and metal rings to connect to your gloves and helmet.

Terry and his *Endeavour* STS-130 crew prepare to board the Astrovan to drive to the launchpad.

Finally, there was a parachute that you wore like a backpack. We also used leather boots, just like the kind that fighter pilots wear. And we wear a diaper because we are in that spacesuit for five or more hours until we get into space—it's a long time before we can use a bathroom. Different spaceships use different spacesuits, but they are all similar.

After getting suited up, we drove out to the rocket in a vehicle called the Astrovan. We plugged the spacesuit into a portable cooling unit that cycled cold water through our suits. Otherwise we would overheat! When we got to *Endeavour*, our space shuttle, we unplugged from the Astrovan, walked to an elevator, went up to the top of the launchpad, and crawled into the shuttle. As soon as we got strapped into the seats, with parachutes on and seatbelts fastened, we plugged into the shuttle's cooling water. By that time I was sweating, because moving around in that bulky suit was hard work, even for just a few minutes. I still remember how good that cold water felt!

Then we waited.

And waited.

And waited.

How many g-forces do you feel during launch?

One g is the force we feel pulling us down toward the ground as we go about our daily life here on the planet, and it's due to Earth's gravity. If you were moving very fast, like in a sports car or airplane or even a rocket, you would feel more g-forces as you turned or accelerated. The fastest sports cars and best fighter jets can accelerate forward about 1 g, the same acceleration we feel from gravity, only moving you forward or side to side and not down.

During my space shuttle launch, at first *Endeavour* accelerated upward at about 1.75 g's. As we continued up into space, the shuttle's acceleration increased to 3 g's! At 1 g, your acceleration is about 10 m (33 ft) per second, every second. So at 3 g's, we were adding about 30 m (98 ft) per second to the shuttle's speed, EVERY SECOND! That is a lot of acceleration! The world's fastest cars can only do that for a few seconds. The shuttle took eight and a half minutes to get onto orbit. That is a lot of acceleration for a long time, which is why we ended up flying at more than 27,000 kmh (almost 16,800 mph), or 8 km (5 mi) per second! That's the speed you need in order to get onto low Earth orbit.

I was strapped in for about three hours before launch in both the space shuttle and the Russian Soyuz rocket. While we were waiting, I told jokes so my crewmates would laugh and not get too nervous. My biggest fear wasn't worrying about the shuttle crashing, but about me making a mistake during launch. I knew everyone was nervous in their own ways, so I tried to do my best to keep my crew loose.

FLYING THE SHUTTLE

The space shuttle had special controls for the commander and pilot to be able to fly it during launch, when it was on orbit, and during landing.

However, the first eight and a half minutes of flight were very, very sensitive, because even a few small errors in flying would make it impossible for us to get into a useful orbit. So manual control by the pilots was just a backup plan in case the shuttle's computers didn't work. But manual control was only possible after the first 90 seconds of flight, because the air pressure was so great during that time while the shuttle was still at low altitudes that only computers had the precision required to fly. Thankfully, the computers always worked during space shuttle launches and the crew never had to take over and fly manually.

If pilots did have to take control manually after 90 seconds after liftoff, we could move the throttles

Who is "Houston"?

You always hear the astronauts talking to "Houston" in space movies. Houston, Texas, is the location of NASA's Johnson Space Center, where astronauts live and train. It is also the home of mission control.

Every American human space mission since 1965 has been controlled out of the Mission Control Center in Houston (MCC, or MCC-H). Mission control is made up of a room of between five and twenty people, called flight controllers, who are responsible for every piece of a mission. The flight director is in charge of the entire flight control team, including the CAPCOM, or Capsule Communicator. When astronauts talk to "Houston," they're talking to the CAPCOM and the team in mission control, in Houston (MCC, or MCC-H).

forward and backward to control the rocket thrust, and
also pitch, yaw, and roll the shuttle, to make sure it was

headed in the right
direction.

Other rockets used for
crewed missions, like the
Russian Soyuz, SpaceX
Falcon 9/Dragon, and
Boeing Starliner capsule
and Atlas V rocket, are completely automated and the
astronauts inside can't fly them manually during launch.
Because I am a pilot, I really preferred the space shuttle
because it was designed for people to fly it, even if only as
a backup plan.

MISSION CONTROL

Every country with a space program has a Mission Control
Center, or MCC. The one in the United States is in Houston,
Texas. Russia's is in Korolev, a town near Moscow. The
Japanese, Europeans, and Canadians each have a Mission
Control Center, and, in fact, some countries have several.

The United States has a big Payload Operations Center in Huntsville, Alabama, where they control the science experiments done on the ISS. We also have several control centers for satellites, the most famous of which is at the Jet Propulsion Laboratory (JPL) in California.

All MCCs have some things in common. First, there is one person in charge of the mission. In Houston, that person is called the flight director. For human missions, there is a CAPCOM, who is the person who talks on the radio to the astronauts in space. At first this stood for Capsule Communicator, but we kept the acronym even when we were flying the space shuttle. Now astronauts launch in capsules from Florida like in the 1960s, so I

guess it makes sense again! There are also several other engineers in MCC-Houston called flight controllers.

They each sit at a special console with a specific name to watch the data from their system. Some of those flight controller names are FDO ("fie-dough," makes sure the vehicle flies in the right direction during launch and landing), ECLSS ("eee-kliss," makes sure the spaceship's water and cooling systems work), CATO ("kay-toe," makes sure the communication gear works), EVA ("ee-vee-ay," in charge of spacewalks), ODIN ("oh-din," makes sure the computers work), OPSPLAN ("ops plan," manages the crew's work schedule). There are also several other flight controllers who work in MCC-Houston.

NASA had its first Flight Control Room, or FCR ("fick-er"), in Florida for the early Mercury missions, but it quickly moved to Houston and has been there ever since the early 1960s. Many of the flight controllers today use the same acronyms and have the same jobs as they did in the early days.

THE DANGERS OF SPACE

Although most human space missions are safe, launching into space and then coming back to Earth is still a dangerous business, and there are occasional accidents.

There have been several fatal accidents since humans began to fly into space. The most famous was in 1986, during the space shuttle program, when the *Challenger* exploded a little more than a minute after launch. One of its solid rocket motors had a leak that let hot gas out. The leak happened because the temperature at launch was below freezing, and an important seal became brittle, allowing hot exhaust to escape through a hole in the side of the rocket.

Unfortunately that leak was pointed right at the shuttle's big orange fuel tank. After a few seconds,

Space shuttle *Challenger* crew, mission 51-L.

it burned through and blew up the tank along with everything else. The NASA astronauts inside *Challenger* didn't have an escape pod or ejection seats or anything that could have helped them. They didn't even have spacesuits on, because NASA thought that the shuttle would be so safe they wouldn't need them.

After that accident NASA made improvements, so by the time I flew on *Endeavour* we had pressure suits to help us survive if we had a really big air leak. We also had parachutes, so that if there was a problem and we couldn't make it to a runway we could at least bail out and parachute down to Earth.

There have been several other fatal space accidents. The first Soyuz capsule crashed in 1967 after its parachute did not open. A few years later in 1971, another Soyuz capsule had a valve accidentally open before it should have, and the atmosphere leaked out of the capsule into space, killing the three cosmonauts inside. At that time, the Soviet Union was also sending its cosmonauts into space without spacesuits to protect them from air leaks.

NASA had an accident during the Apollo Moon program where there was a fire on the launchpad during a practice training session in 1967. Also, the space shuttle *Columbia* was hit by a piece of foam from its fuel tank about a minute after liftoff in 2003. That put a big hole in the wing that the crew didn't know about, and two weeks later when they came back to Earth the wing burned off during re-entry and the shuttle crashed.

As horrible as these accidents were, they are rare and most people who travel into space return to Earth safely.

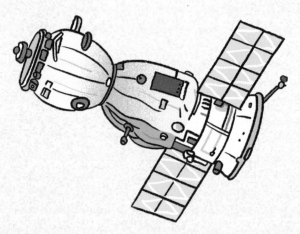

Soyuz capsule.

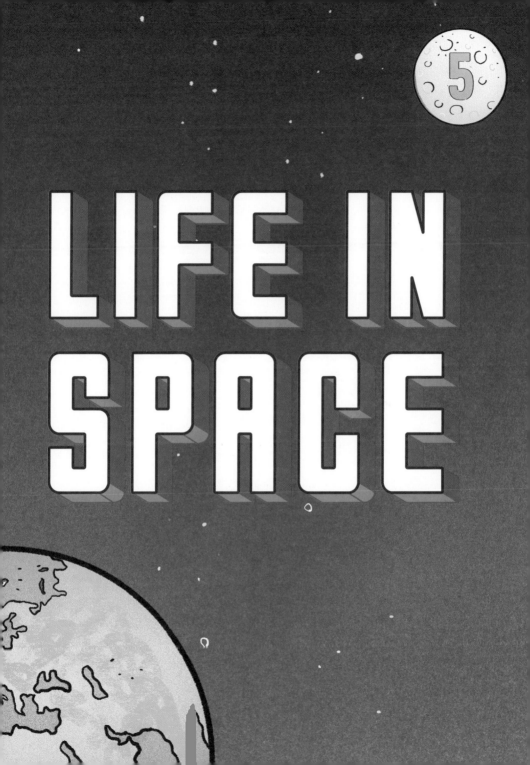

EVERYTHING IS HARDER IN SPACE

All astronauts have to learn many things about living in space that are very different from living on Earth. That was true for the early astronauts back in the 1960s, it's true for today's ISS astronauts, and it will be true for people who fly into space in the future. Things like how you float in weightlessness, how you go to the bathroom, how you eat and drink, how you work and keep track of

Terry floating in the US Lab on his 100th day in space.

your things. We have a saying that "everything is harder in space" (except pull-ups!). Living in space is very exciting, but it can also be challenging. It is an adventure unlike anything on Earth.

My first space mission was about two weeks on the space shuttle, and my second mission was about 200 days on the ISS. Those are pretty typical mission

Cosmonaut Valery Polyakov

durations. American astronauts have spent up to 355 days in space, and the Russians have had several cosmonauts stay for longer than that. The person with the longest space mission ever was Valery Polyakov, who was on the Mir space station for 438 days!

That was a very long mission and when he got back to Earth he felt very weak, though he was eventually able to recover. My friend and ISS crewmate Gennady Padalka has spent more than 879 days in space during his five spaceflights, the most total time in space of any human!

What's the best part of being an astronaut?

Ask an Astronaut

The best part of being an astronaut is getting to see the planet and universe from space. Our planet is so amazing and there are so many billions of stars out there. I would love to go back to space if all I had to do was take pictures of the universe.

Floating was also fun. I loved feeling like Superman! It is amazing to just float, looking down at the floor and not falling, even though it feels like you're falling. It is something that you can't really do on Earth, and it took me weeks before I was really good at it.

Another really fun part of being an astronaut is training for a mission. Most astronauts will say that flying in space is the best part, but I also enjoyed training for my spaceflights. That meant I had a spaceflight to look forward to! They say that every astronaut's favorite mission is their next one, no matter how many times they've flown before!

The Gulf of Aden (between Yemen and the Arabian Sea) from space.

CHALLENGES OF LIVING IN SPACE

There are two big problems that limit how long people can live in space. The first is the effect of weightlessness on bones and muscles. Luckily the ISS has shown us that people can live and work in space for a long time as long as they exercise and take vitamin D. If astronauts were on a planet like Mars or even on the Moon, there would be some gravity that would help their bones and muscles, and this would not be as big of an issue as it is in the weightlessness of orbit.

Floating like Superman during STS-130.

The other big problem astronauts face in space is radiation (waves or particles of energy), and that is much trickier. When radiation comes in from our Sun or other stars far out in the galaxy, it can damage human tissue and sometimes cause cancer. Luckily, Earth has a magnetic field around our whole planet. That is like a force field that blocks most of the harmful radiation. In fact, we probably wouldn't have any life on Earth if we didn't have this protective magnetic field. But when astronauts travel more than a 1,000 km (620 mi) above Earth, they lose the protection of the magnetic field, and radiation becomes a big problem. The longest that astronauts have lived in the high-radiation environment of deep space has been less than two weeks. That was during the Apollo Moon missions. We don't know how long humans will be able to survive in deep space, but we should find some ways to minimize astronauts' exposure to radiation. We could block some radiation with shielding, like surrounding the spaceship with water tanks. Or we could have them spend less time in deep-space radiation by building rocket engines that get them to their destination faster.

How do you go to the bathroom in space?

Ask an Astronaut

This is probably the most common question asked of every astronaut. And it's a good question because it's one thing that every astronaut has to know perfectly before they fly into space on their first mission.

The main differences between space toilets and Earth toilets are that space toilets use airflow instead of gravity to keep things moving in the correct direction, and they don't use water to flush.

A space toilet is divided into two parts: a hose for number one, and a bucket that you sit on for number two. The hose has a funnel on its end that you pee into. The bucket has a lid that opens, and after you have done your business you close it. It was the pilot's job on shuttle missions to make sure the toilet was clean, and I was very proud as the pilot on mission STS-130 that I had the cleanest toilet in the history of the space shuttle program. That was my story, anyway.

EATING IN SPACE

Eating was one of my favorite things to do in space. There were several types of food that we ate. First, there were packages similar to what people in the military eat. NASA calls this irradiated food, and the military calls them Meals Ready to Eat (MRE). They are green bags of meat or soup or vegetables or desserts or whatever. You just open them and eat them with no cooking required, though you can heat them up if you want. My favorite food of this type was minestrone soup. And chocolate pudding cake.

The next food type is called rehydratable. This comes in a clear plastic bag, and it is dehydrated so it's hard and crunchy. We plug this bag into a machine, select how many

milliliters of water to add, select cool or hot water, and press a button. The food bag is filled with water, and we mash it around and wait ten minutes for it to get fully rehydrated. I would also swing it around in a circle, like a centrifuge, to fully mix the water. And voilà—dinner! Just like the irradiated food, rehydratable food could also be meat or vegetables or fruits or desserts. The turkey, spinach, scrambled eggs, and sausage patties were some of my favorites.

Another type of food was just normal canned or packaged food straight from the grocery store. Some examples of this are chocolate (like peanut butter cups), beef jerky, bags of tuna, and bags of olives. This type of food was easy because it was in the same packages you find at the store on Earth. NASA also took off-the-shelf food like crackers, candy, and cookies and packaged them in vacuum-sealed clear plastic bags. One example of this was a popular candy of round chocolate-covered pieces, although NASA called them "chocolate-covered candies" because they didn't want to promote the brand-name version.

In addition to NASA food, I also had Russian and European food. The Russian food came in its own special packages and we had to use a Russian machine to fill their food bags with water. They had great soup (called borscht) and fish (in cans, like tuna cans) and mashed potatoes. The Europeans had very fancy food that was prepared by a real chef. One item that I liked was a French dish called duck confit. That was something that I never had on Earth.

Drinks come in silver bags. They are full of powder and you just add water to make fruit drinks, milk, coffee, tea, sports drinks, and smoothies. Basically any drink that you can make from powder. My favorites were hot chocolate and also sports drinks.

Most astronauts say that shrimp cocktail is their favorite food. That may be because it's spicy, and most astronauts lose some of their sense of taste while in space (thanks to gravity's impact on congestion and our bodies' ability to taste and smell), so we tend to like spicy foods. I personally liked any kind of chocolate, including brownies, chocolate pudding cake, or just candy. And don't worry, your senses return to normal when you touch back down on Earth.

Can you grow your own food in space?

Ask an Astronaut

Yes, you can, but it is difficult and requires a lot of energy, nutrients, and water. Water and soil are very heavy, and that makes them expensive to launch onto orbit. So NASA has found that it is easier and cheaper to send up food from Earth than it is to have astronauts grow their own food while they're in space. That is OK when we are flying on low Earth orbit: But when we start sending astronauts out into deep space to live permanently, they will need to be able to grow their own food. Over the past few years, astronauts have grown red romaine lettuce, green lettuce, Chinese cabbage, lentils, radishes, and mustard greens. That would make a nice salad. But these types of food would only meet some of astronauts' nutritional needs. They would still need proteins and grains that come from things like meat, dairy products, nuts, and wheat.

Most crops on Earth require hundreds of liters of water to make 1 kg (2.2 lb) of food. Even though much of that water could be recycled in space, it is still a lot. To launch a single liter of water can cost tens of thousands of dollars, so it is cheaper to launch food that is already cooked. Another problem with growing your own crops in space is that if there is a problem and the food doesn't grow properly, the astronauts could be without food and starve.

SLEEPING IN SPACE

I was very nervous before my first space mission that I wouldn't be able to sleep in space. But once I got onto orbit, I didn't have any problems at all sleeping! I was so tired every night that I closed my eyes and fell right asleep.

When I was on *Endeavour*, there were six of us and we all slept on the middeck, which is a room about half the size of a small bedroom. We each picked out a spot on the wall or ceiling or floor and attached our sleeping bag and slept there. I had an iPod for music and a blindfold and ear plugs to help me sleep on the bright and noisy space shuttle. I also brought my clothes for the next morning into my sleeping bag. That way when I woke up I didn't have to look for them, and I could quickly get dressed right there in my sleeping bag. Spending time looking for things is a real problem in space, and little things like keeping your clothes with you really help.

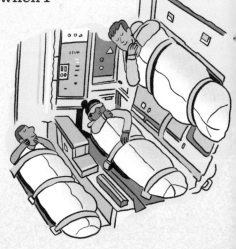

Do astronauts ever get sick in space?

Sicknesses like the common cold or flu don't really happen in space. Our doctors are very careful to make sure we aren't sick when we leave Earth, and all of our equipment is cleaned, so it is very unlikely that an astronaut would come into contact with bad bacteria or viruses while in space.

One very common problem astronauts deal with is back pain. Back pain probably happens because astronauts grow and get taller by a few centimeters in weightlessness. Without the force of gravity pushing me down, I grew 5 cm (2 in) after two weeks in space. After I stopped growing, the pain stopped. A few hours after being back on Earth, I was back to my normal height.

Another common problem that many astronauts have comes from carbon dioxide (CO_2) in the air. The CO_2 level on the space station is at least ten times higher than on Earth. That extra CO_2 can give astronauts headaches, make them dizzy, crabby, and even confused.

ASTRONAUT ACTIVITY

You've practiced weightlessness already. But now you can try to practice floating.

With a parent's permission, and following all the rules of the place you're going to, find a body of water where you have enough room to move, like a pool. (The bathtub might be too small!)

1. Lie on your back in the water until your body is floating. Sometimes this is challenging. Your legs may sink until you're standing upright again, or your head may tip back so far you flip over.

2. Practice finding the right balance. Then, when you're floating, close your eyes and imagine that you are in space, floating in the middle of the ISS.

On the ISS, I had my own sleeping quarters. It was the size of a bathroom stall. I kept my laptop, family pictures, snacks and water bags, and a few days worth of clothes stuffed under bungee cords. The best part of my crew quarters was that I didn't have to attach my sleeping bag to the wall. I could just float while I slept! I would climb into my sleeping bag, get my arms and head completely inside, turn off the lights, and float. It was so cool! As soon as I closed my eyes, I couldn't tell which way was up or down—I was just floating in space.

Sometimes I listened to music while I slept. The Russian crew psychologist sent us some sounds from Earth, like rain, waves at a beach, jungle noises, and sounds from a crowded café. Every night for a month, I fell asleep to the sound of rain. Until then I had been having dreams of floating in space. But when I started listening to sounds from Earth while I slept, my dreams started to be of places on Earth. I would dream of running across grass fields or being in buildings and seeing familiar people and animals.

COMMUNICATING WITH EARTH

The hardest thing about being in space for so long was being separated from my friends and family. My longest mission lasted more than six months, and that was a long time to be away from them. Luckily there are several different ways for astronauts on the ISS to communicate with people on Earth. First, there is an email system that works just like email on Earth—with one exception: The email only gets sent and received when the ISS is in view of one of our special communication satellites. This happens most of the time, but not *all* of the time.

There is also a phone system that works through those same communication satellites. When we have a good connection, astronauts can call anywhere on Earth, but nobody can call us. Unfortunately the connection suddenly cuts off as we fly around the planet and lose contact with the satellites, which happens every 30 to 40 minutes, so sometimes you have to talk fast!

In addition to phone and email, there is a video conference system similar to Zoom or Skype or FaceTime that we can use for work or for connecting with our families. It requires a small team on the ground to set up, so we can't just say "let's do a quick Zoom call"—they have to be scheduled in advance. Also, the person on the ground needs special equipment. It was worth the extra effort for these video calls to be able to see people's faces, because 200 days was a long time to go without seeing my friends and family in person. Unfortunately there is no way to come home quickly if there were a family emergency on Earth, and you would only be able to talk with them using one of these methods.

There are other things about living in space that are difficult. For me a big one was keeping track of things. Everything is floating, so you can't just put something down on the table, because it will quickly float away! So if you are carrying a pen or wrench or notebook or food, you constantly have to keep track of it. You have to keep things in your pocket, in a plastic bag, on a tether, or attached to Velcro. Otherwise they will float away and disappear. It took me a few weeks until I was really good at organizing my stuff and having it ready to use, without losing it.

What time zone do you use in space?

Ask an Astronaut

The ISS flies around Earth so fast that it moves across sixteen time zones every hour. To keep up with that, you'd need to change the time on your watch every four minutes! No astronaut wants to be glued to their watch, so we came up with a different way to keep track of time. We use Universal Time Coordinated (UTC), which is also known around the world as Greenwich Mean Time (GMT).

Greenwich was a town near London, England, before it became a part of London itself, and it is home to the British Royal Observatory. For centuries the British government used this place to study the motion of the stars and planets.

Because the observatory at Greenwich was so accurate, GMT was the common time used for science or military operations everywhere since the days of the British Empire, and the ISS was no different. Astronauts set their watches to GMT, and their daily schedule is based on GMT. Using GMT as a common time reference makes things simple for astronauts and engineers all over the world.

TEAMWORK IN SPACE

Most astronauts get along very well with their crewmates. One of the most important things that NASA looks for when they hire new astronauts is their ability to spend a long time with a small group of people in a small space, because that is what they will have to do on a space station mission. When I was reviewing applications for people who wanted to become NASA astronauts, their ability to get along with others was the most important thing I looked for. It is very important for

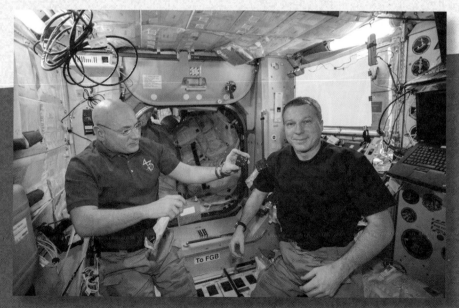

Terry sharing a brownie with Scott Kelly in Node 1 on the ISS.

astronauts on long-duration space missions to maintain good relationships with their crewmates, because if some crewmates aren't getting along with each other it negatively impacts the mission.

Spending time with my crewmates was one of the most fun things I did during my time in space. I especially liked hanging out in the Service Module on the Russian segment with the crew. It was a chance for us to eat dinner together and laugh, watch TV, listen to music, and tell stories. It was also a chance for my Russian cosmonaut friends to teach me new words in the Russian language. I'm still learning Russian today, even years after I left NASA!

But just like anyone on Earth, sometimes astronauts need to spend some time alone. The ISS is really good

for this because it is a big place, and everyone has their own small room where they can have privacy, put up family pictures, and just get away. There are rules on the space station just like there are rules on Earth.

When fifteen nations got together to build the ISS, they came up with something called the Intergovernmental Agreement, which tells how each nation would handle a criminal situation that occurred in space. There is also something called the ISS Crew Code of Conduct, which lays out how each crewmember is supposed to act and

ASTRONAUT ACTIVITY

Find two pieces of paper and something to write with. On one piece of paper, make a list of your closest friends or family who you would like to take to space with you. On the other piece of paper, write down a Crew Code of Conduct, ten rules that every space crew should follow. How will you communicate with each other when you're far from home and in close quarters? Who will be responsible for which chores? And most important, what will you do if there's a disagreement? A code of conduct for you and your friends is a good resource about how to treat others here on Earth, too!

behave. The good news is that in more than twenty years of ISS missions, nothing bad has happened in space that has required us to use these agreements. Astronauts have behaved pretty well.

These international agreements are for very serious problems, and each astronaut or cosmonaut still works for his or her own space agency, each with its own set of rules. So when I was in space, I had NASA bosses back on Earth. And when I was the ISS commander, not only did I have to worry about my NASA bosses, but I also had to consider the other international space agencies in Russia, Canada, Japan, and Europe. Also, Mission Control in Houston (MCC-H) is responsible for directing what happens daily on the space station. MCC-H is generally in charge of the overall mission, but there are also control

centers in Moscow and Europe and Japan and Canada, and they are in charge of their own modules and equipment. There is also a big control center in Huntsville, Alabama, that is in charge of American science experiments, and several others in Europe that are in charge of their science experiments.

On top of it all, each mission has a crew commander on the ISS. I was in space during Expedition 42 with one commander, then when he went back to Earth, our mission changed to Expedition 43 and I became commander. When I went back to Earth, I handed over command of the station to my Russian friend Gennady Padalka, and he was the Expedition 44 commander. This cycle continues every few months. Ultimately it is the commander who is in charge of what happens on the ISS, especially during emergency situations.

WORKING IN SPACE

When I flew on the space shuttle, each astronaut had a very specific job. Some were responsible for doing spacewalks, some had experiments or maintenance to do on the ISS, some were tasked with flying the robotic arm.

ISS missions usually last six months or longer, so every astronaut and cosmonaut has to be trained to do many tasks. There aren't enough people onboard the station to allow each person to be limited to doing only one job. Most ISS missions last so long that every astronaut ends up doing a little bit of everything while they are in space. For example, during my 200-day mission, I operated the robotic arm, did maintenance on a lot of broken equipment, helped perform more than 250 science experiments, did three spacewalks, helped film an IMAX movie, did countless TV and news interviews, helped pack and unpack several cargo ships, was our crew's medical officer, took more photos than any other astronaut and shared them through social media, helped with the Soyuz

Spacewalk selfie.

during launch and landing, performed many medical investigations on my own body, exercised several hours per day, was the ISS commander, and talked to NASA and other space agencies around the world. Doing something different every day was one of the reasons I loved flying in space. I never got bored, and every day was an adventure.

SCIENCE ON THE ISS

During my seven months in space, my crew did more than 250 different experiments from almost every branch of science. Biology, physics, astronomy, medicine, engineering, psychology, materials science, combustion science, and more.

I think one of the most important experiments we are doing in space uses something called AMS-2, or Alpha Magnetic Spectrometer. It is a large white box, about the size of a big refrigerator, that is outside the ISS near the solar arrays. It is looking for very tiny particles, called antimatter, that fly in from all around the universe. Detecting these particles will help physicists and astronomers determine what the universe is made of.

Which planets have you seen?

Ask an Astronaut

Let's start with the Moon. It's not a planet, but it is the most recognizable object in the night sky. When the Moon dropped behind our atmosphere, it looked like it was turning blue and getting squashed, because of something called refraction. This is what it's called when light bends as it travels through matter. This is also why a glass lens can focus light, and if you are on land and look at something underwater it looks funny. Our atmosphere makes the Moon look flat, and it was really cool to see it getting squashed.

In terms of seeing actual planets, Jupiter was the most impressive. It is the biggest planet and it looked orange and very bright. Saturn was yellow, and a little less bright because it is smaller and farther away. Mars was very red. Venus was also one of the brightest objects in the sky, because it is the closest planet to Earth. It looked white and yellow.

One of the most interesting things I saw in space was Mercury. Because it is so close to the Sun, you can only see it right before sunrise or after sunset. Most people on Earth live in places where there are buildings and trees that normally block the view of Mercury, so they never see it. In space there was nothing blocking my view, so I had a chance to see the hottest planet in the solar system.

We also have equipment on the ISS that allows us to burn different types of fuels and materials. That is helping scientists understand the basics of combustion, which is very important because cars and airplanes use combustion to burn fuel. If we can make that process a little more efficient, we could save a lot of gas and help the environment. I did another experiment called the Capillary Flow Experiment, or CFE. It was a big clear jar of goo, and as I rotated a flat spatula inside the jar, the goo would shoot up to the top of the jar because of the changing shape of the container. That was really fascinating to see, and it could help spacecraft engineers develop better fuel tanks so they can use every drop of fuel just by rotating the wall inside the tank.

The science that I spent the most time on was studying my own body. I measured my weight, took my blood pressure, measured my physical fitness level on an exercise bike, did ultrasound scans of my eyes and brain and heart, did infrared and laser scans of my eyeballs, measured the pressure in my eyeballs, measured my lung capacity, took computer tests that measured if my brain was working normally or more slowly, and measured how strong I was at weightlifting. I even kept a journal so psychologists could see how I was feeling emotionally throughout my mission. NASA and many other scientists are very interested in seeing how space affects all aspects of our bodies. I think one of the best scientific accomplishments of the ISS has been to show that people can live and work for a long time in space.

SUPPORTING LIFE IN SPACE

The ISS gets its electrical power from the Sun through big solar arrays. These giant solar arrays rotate in two directions, using an "alpha" joint to match the station's movement around Earth (4 degrees every minute) and a "beta" joint to track the Sun if it's off to the left or right of the station's orbit. The ISS also has radiators that are used to cool the station down, and they are attached to the solar arrays, but pointed in the opposite direction. This is very helpful because while the solar panels are getting direct sunlight, the radiators are pointed away from the Sun so they can cool down.

Solar arrays on ISS.

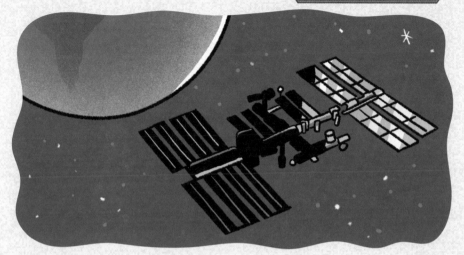

ISS on orbit around Earth.

Electricity is the only thing we make in space. Everything else has to be brought on supply cargo ships from Earth. Electrical power is necessary to run the station. The station has batteries to provide electricity when the ISS is in Earth's shadow, a condition we call eclipse. Each orbit takes about 93 minutes, and the ISS is in sunlight for somewhere between 50 and 93 minutes of each orbit, and the batteries are used between 30 and 40 minutes of each orbit. Luckily the Sun won't stop working for a long, long time.

But if the solar panels completely stopped working, the batteries would only last a few orbits before they were drained, like an electric car that wasn't plugged in, and the

ISS would lose power. The good news is that those solar arrays really can't stop working. As long as some sunlight shines on them, they will produce electricity.

The outside of the ISS gets really, really hot when the Sun shines directly on it, and really really cold when it is on the night side of Earth with no sunlight. The temperature can go from +120°C (250°F) to -160°C (-320°F)! There are two basic systems to keep the inside of the station at a normal temperature so the astronauts are safe: a cooling system for the inside of the station where people live and a different cooling system on the outside of the station.

The ISS orbiting high up in sunlight while the Sun has set on Earth down below.

The ISS is not in the freezing cold shade long enough to need a large heating system.

There are several water loops that run through the inside of the station, behind the walls. They have cold water to cool down equipment. This cooling system also has fans that blow air over the water, which cools the air, keeping the temperature comfortable for the crew. When I was there we kept the temperature about 22°C (71.6°F), just like in my house here on Earth.

Once that cool water takes heat out of the equipment and the air, it warms up. That warm water then flows over a different loop of ammonia fluid. Ammonia is a very efficient coolant, but it is also a deadly chemical, so we have lots of precautions to make sure it doesn't leak into the crew cabin. The ammonia takes heat from the water loop on the inside of the station and then flows to the radiators that are on the outside of the ISS. As it moves through the radiators, the heat that was in the ammonia gets sent out into space as infrared energy.

ISS cooling system.

Then the ammonia is cold again, and it flows back to the water loops, where the whole process starts again. NASA and our international partners have spent a lot of effort making sure the station has the right equipment to keep its temperature not too hot, and not too cold, but just right.

STEERING THE ISS

There are two ways to maneuver the ISS while in space. The first is to make it point in different directions. This is called rotation. The second is to move it to make it go faster or slower, which makes it climb or descend. That's called translation. Both ways require very different equipment to make them happen.

First, let's talk about rotation. The main way the ISS rotates is by using Control Moment Gyros (CMGs). The ISS has four massive metal rings that weigh more than 100 kg (220 lb) each and spin more than 6,000 times per minute, or 100 revolutions each second. That spinning is called "angular momentum," and when the ISS needs to change the direction it is pointing, a computer commands an electric motor to push against those CMGs, which then

ASTRONAUT ACTIVITY

Try this experiment to help you understand how CMGs work:

1 Hold the front wheel of your bicycle off the ground while the rear wheel stays on the ground.

2 Spin the front wheel as fast as you can.

3 Now try to turn the wheel left or right while it's off the ground and spinning.

You will feel the bike try to rotate in a different direction. This is because of something called angular momentum and gyroscopic torque. That means if you try to move something that is spinning, it will resist that motion by moving itself in a different direction.

push the ISS to point in the right direction. CMGs are used on many satellites and are a very efficient way to control spaceships, but they do need some thrusters to help them out. The ISS has a set of small rocket thrusters on the Russian segment that can also be used to point the station in different directions.

Translation is a very different maneuver, and it occurs when those same small Russian rocket thrusters fire, making the station speed up. The ISS could turn around backward, and use those rockets to slow down, but we rarely do that. There is a very thin atmosphere at the ISS orbital altitude. As the ISS flies through the thin air, it gives a constant drag on the station. This slows it down a very small amount every day, so every few months the rocket engines fire to speed us back up.

In order to climb on orbit, you need to speed up, and in order to descend, you need to slow down. This means that whenever the ISS needs to climb, we fire the rockets to speed up. Like translation, climbing is often used to overcome Earth's atmospheric drag. But it's also sometimes used when we need to maneuver to avoid space junk or debris, or if we need to adjust our orbit slightly

Do things burn in space?

It is very difficult for something to burn in weightlessness, for two main reasons. First of all, most things in space are fireproof. They wouldn't even burn on Earth! But the really interesting reason is because there is no convection in space. Convection is when hot air is less dense than cool air and it rises. This happens on Earth because of gravity, which pulls heavier things down and lets lighter things go up. When there is a fire on Earth, convection makes the air blow from the bottom to the top, which constantly brings fresh oxygen to the fire. However, in space lighter things do not go up, so there is no convection to bring new oxygen to fires. They naturally burn themselves out.

Astronauts have done combustion experiments in space, and they've found that flames burn in spheres, or balls, because of the lack of convection.

to meet up with a cargo or crew ship that is coming to rendezvous with us.

ANIMALS IN SPACE

The first animal to make it onto orbit was a dog named Laika. She flew on the second Soviet satellite, called Sputnik-2, in 1957. Unfortunately she did not survive and come back to Earth because her spaceship did not have a re-entry heat shield or parachute, but her mission was very important because she proved that animals could fly into and survive in space. A few years later, two more Soviet dogs, Belka and Strelka, became the first two mammals to make it onto orbit and successfully return to Earth. They were big heroes in the Soviet Union and are still very famous today in Russia, with their own exhibit at the Memorial Museum of Cosmonautics in Moscow.

Americans also flew animals into space during the early years of space flight, including several monkeys named Gordo, Able, and Baker. A chimpanzee named

Ham became very famous in 1961 because he was smart enough to pull levers and do things that human astronauts would have to do while they were in space. He was a celebrity in America because he flew right before Alan Shepard became the first American in space. Another famous early animal in space was Félicette, a French cat who flew in 1963 and then successfully parachuted back to Earth.

Unfortunately we have not had pets on the ISS yet, though hopefully one day we will. For now, there is no place on the station to take a dog for a walk or set up a cat litter box, and dogs would have a hard time playing fetch in weightlesness.

The animals who have been to space have been very important for science and helping humans. Some have shown that flying into space is possible, and others have helped with medical and other experiments. The most common animals on the ISS are mice. They are very confused their first few days in space, because they float around unsure of what to do. But then they get used to weightlessness and start to run around their cages, as though they are in a spinning wheel on Earth. Mice are very important to our science program because they help us develop better medicines to improve human health care on Earth. Other interesting types of animals that have flown on the ISS and space shuttle include spiders, fruit flies, frogs, butterflies, and worms, among others.

SPACE TRASH

We do not have recycling in space like we do on Earth. There isn't a special container to put plastics or glass or metal or paper in. Instead, we divide our trash into two types—dry trash and wet trash. The way we get rid of trash in space is to pack it into designated cargo vehicles. There is a cargo ship leaving the ISS every few months. Most of those burn up in the atmosphere above the Pacific Ocean, but the SpaceX Dragon cargo vehicle has a heat shield and parachute, so it is recovered when it comes back to Earth and splashes down safely. We don't put too much trash in those because they are full of science experiments that need to come back to Earth.

Although we don't recycle in space the way we do on Earth, we do a different but very important kind of recycling—reclaiming water. The Russian and American segments of the ISS have a system that takes humidity out of the air and recycles that water. They both have systems that remove carbon dioxide from the atmosphere, but the American system can use that carbon dioxide to

SpaceX Dragon cargo ship, taken from the ISS.

Can you play Minecraft or other video games on the ISS?

There have been some video games on the space station, but not a lot, because there are a lot of restrictions. One big problem with playing video games on the ISS is that there isn't a good internet connection. Also, there are a lot of restrictions about which programs we are allowed to have on the computers in space, so each game would have to be scanned and tested to make sure it didn't have viruses and would be safe on the station's computers. But if you really want to play video games, and have one that doesn't need the internet, you can do it.

recycle it. There is also a system that recycles urine from the bathroom to turn it into water. We then use a special process called electrolysis that sends electricity into the water to turn it into hydrogen and oxygen. The oxygen is useful for breathing, and the hydrogen is combined with the carbon dioxide to make more water. The system is very complicated and requires a lot of maintenance to keep it running. It has also been used to develop water filters down here on Earth to help isolated people who don't have clean water in their villages.

Recycling water is very important because it is very heavy, and it costs tens of thousands of dollars per kilogram for NASA to launch supplies to the ISS, so recycling this precious resource saves a lot of money. Also, when we go to live on the Moon or Mars for long periods of time, we will have to recycle water. The ISS is a good place to learn how to perfect this important skill.

My absolute favorite thing to do in space was to look out of the window and down at our planet. There was so much to see, and even though I was in space for more than seven months, I never got tired of seeing that view. I got to know Earth by colors, because every country and ocean has their own unique shades and colors. I saw city lights at night that showed me where wealth was on our planet. I saw a beautiful planet but also one that has some big environmental problems. Most of all I saw my home, the home of all humans, flying through space on an amazing journey around our Sun and through our galaxy.

During the daytime, you can't tell that there are people on Earth unless you look closely. I could see airplane contrails, which are the long white trails that look like clouds or smoke coming out of jet engines, coming from some crowded places like New York or London. I could also see a lot of airplanes flying there, but most places on Earth did not have contrails. Large ships sometimes made a wake that was visible, with long stretches of waves behind the boat. And in large harbors I could sometimes see very large boats at anchor, just off shore. I could see the concrete buildings of big cities like London or Buenos Aires or Los Angeles, but for the most part someone who is in space would not notice people on Earth during the day. But at night, it's a much different story.

At night you can see city lights, and there are a lot of them. I could also see red flares from oil and gas fields. One of the most interesting things I saw at night were fishing boats, because some fishermen use bright floodlights to attract fish to the surface at night. In places like Japan, Korea, and Argentina, they are white or light blue, but the boats near Thailand are bright green. That was really cool to see hundreds of green dots in the ocean.

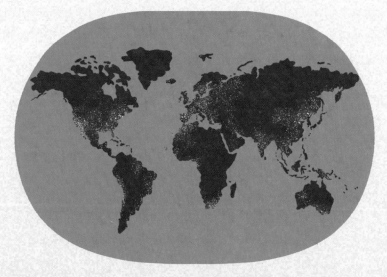

You can see bright city lights at night from space.

What was it like to look out of the Cupola?

The Cupola is a seven-window module on the bottom of the ISS where you can look down and see our planet or look up and see the stars. I installed it on my first space mission, STS-130.

The whole crew was amazed when we opened the window covers for the first time. The view of Earth was beautiful. A few hours later, the whole inside of the space station turned red and pink. That was really unexpected. We were flying over Australia at the time. The western part of Australia, called the Outback, is very red, because there is a lot of iron in the soil. And there was so much light reflecting off the red Earth below that it turned the inside of the ISS red!

The Cupola is every astronaut's favorite place to spend time because the view is so spectacular. I spent countless hours there during my seven months on the ISS, and I wish I could spend more time there enjoying the view.

During my first spaceflight, I was watching Earth go by one night, looking at city lights, when something very important struck me. When I saw cities at night, I wasn't looking at how many people were down there. I was seeing how wealthy they were. Regions with the most wealth, like America, Europe, and eastern Asia, had lots and lots of lights. But poor regions like Africa or South America had much less light, even though there were a lot of people there. That really made an impression on me, to be in outer space and be able to see where wealth was on Earth by where there were city lights.

SIGHTSEEING FROM SPACE

The problem with being an astronaut is that you see so many amazing places on our planet that you want to visit. It's hard to pick just one as my favorite.

I loved seeing deserts. The bright red Outback in Australia. The orange-red Sahara Desert in northern Africa. The massive, beige-pink Saudi desert. The fascinating Namib Desert in southern Africa, home to the world's largest sand dunes. In fact, those sand dunes

ASTRONAUT ACTIVITY

What are the most impressive places you've seen here on Earth? The Grand Canyon? The Rocky Mountains? Now, what do you think might look most impressive from space? The Himalayas, maybe the Nile Delta, or the massive splashes of light from your favorite cities? Mark the places Terry mentions on a map and then mark the places on Earth you would like to see from space. There are no wrong answers!

Here's a list to get you started:

The Grand Canyon, The Egyptian pyramids, Mount Everest.

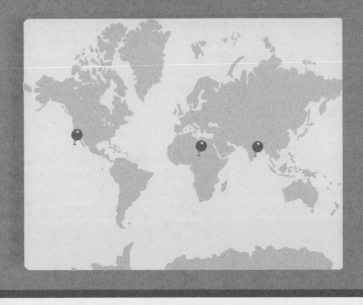

are so tall that I could easily see them from space! And there was always a big cloud just off the west coast of Namibia that looked like it had been there forever, in the Atlantic Ocean.

I loved seeing thousands and thousands of kilometers of white snow, ice, and clouds. Canada and Russia were always covered in white, wrapping almost around the entire planet. The oceans of the world were also very interesting, each one a different shade of blue. They all have fascinating islands. Some of those islands are rocky, like Hawaii, the Galapagos, and the Azores. Some are a beautiful shade of turquoise and aqua blue. The Pacific Ocean has a lot of islands made of coral reefs called atolls.

What do storms look like from space?

I had a chance to see twenty-three different hurricanes and tropical storms from space. They are all in the shape of a spiral, and they spin in a counterclockwise direction in the Northern Hemisphere and a clockwise direction in the Southern Hemisphere.

The most interesting part of a hurricane is the eye, the center of the storm. The more defined and perfectly circular the eye, the more powerful the storm.

Thunderstorms are also amazing sights. I was always fascinated to look down at Earth at night over South America, Africa, or the South Pacific, and see long lines of thunderstorms that stretched for hundreds of miles. Sometimes these storms are so powerful that the flashes from the lightning illuminate the inside of the space station. It was amazing to think that a storm on Earth could light up a spaceship in space.

Typhoon Maysak.

After you've been in space for a month or two, you start to get very familiar with Earth. I could look out and tell if I was over Canada or Europe or North Africa or Australia, just by looking at the colors and the weather. It was fun to get to know our planet by colors—the blues of the ocean, the whites of Canadian and Russian snow and ice, the red and pink and orange of the deserts. The jungles of the Amazon in South America and the Congo in Africa were very dark. Clouds, no matter where they were, were really bright. The North Pacific had really unique storms that were huge and looked like galaxies, with skinny, curved bands of clouds. And eastern Canada had really strange swirls of white that were difficult to tell if they were ice or clouds.

I spent a lot of time taking pictures of Earth, and I always wanted to know where I was when I took the picture.

Luckily when I was a kid I loved geography, and I always had a map or an atlas nearby. So when I got to space, I already knew how to find a lot of places and countries and cities. We had an atlas on the ISS, so at night when I was looking through the pictures I had taken that day I would open the atlas and use it to make sure I knew where each picture was from. There is also a special program on our computers on the ISS called World Map. It is sort of like a map app on your phone. It shows you where you are over Earth, and where you will be for the next two orbits. You can use that program to figure out the next time you will pass over the pyramids in Egypt or Mount Everest or the Grand Canyon, in case you want to take pictures.

Although using maps or computers to find my location was fine, I always preferred to know where I was without help, just by recognizing the ground below. And after seven months on orbit, I think I got pretty good at recognizing many places on our beautiful planet.

The Grand Canyon from ISS.

LIGHT SHOWS

There is an amazing thing that appears in the wintertime night sky near the North and South Poles. It usually happens in December, January, and February in the north, and in June, July, and August in the south. It is a very large green light show that can fill the sky, with towering pillars and waves of green and pink and red light that look like a flowing river. People who live in the far north or south have always marveled at these apparitions. Some even thought the green lights were from the spirits of their ancestors. In the Northern Hemisphere, this is called the Aurora Borealis, or northern lights. In the Southern Hemisphere,

it is called Aurora Australis, or southern lights.

Seeing the auroras from space was one of the most beautiful and amazing things I saw. I loved taking

ASTRONAUT ACTIVITY

Depending on where you live, you can see different constellations and the northern or southern lights in the night sky. On a particularly dark night, and with a parent's permission, go outside and see how many constellations you can spot. Here are a few to look for:

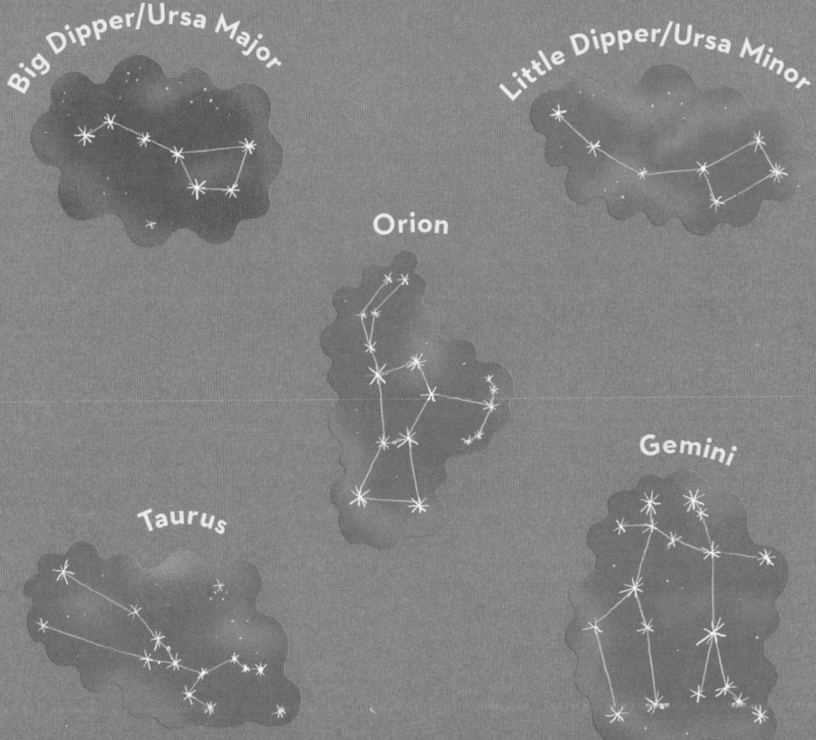

Big Dipper/Ursa Major

Little Dipper/Ursa Minor

Orion

Taurus

Gemini

pictures of them, and one of my favorite scenes in the IMAX film *A Beautiful Planet* is of the southern lights. It looks like a flowing river of green and red plasma, and it is amazing.

The auroras are caused by particles from the Sun. There are massive explosions on the Sun that shoot hundreds of millions of tons of electrons and protons out into space. Sometimes those particles get shot toward our planet, and they arrive here a few days later. Then they get captured by Earth's magnetic field, which is like a big force field circling our planet. We have a magnetic field

Aurora Borealis over the United Kingdom.

Can you see climate change from space?

You can't actually see change from space, at least not in one glance. You need to have a series of pictures taken over many years or even decades to see that kind of change.

However, I did see some environmental problems from space. The most obvious one was smog and pollution over China, which, from space, looks like a giant cloud of yellow and brown haze.

Another environmental problem I saw was deforestation, which is when people cut down large areas of forests. They do this to sell the wood to furniture makers or construction companies, or to clear the land so they can plant crops or raise cattle. I could see a very large area of the Amazon rain forest in Brazil that had been deforested. I also saw the island nation of Madagascar in Africa that was once covered by a rain forest. Today, there is just a small strip of green forest on the eastern part of the island, and the rest is a brown desert. We have lost millions of species of animals over the past few decades because deforestation destroys their habitats. Deforestation is also a problem because trees help take carbon dioxide out of the air, which we really need to help slow down climate change.

ASTRONAUT ACTIVITY

Do something about climate change in your neighborhood today. Here are some ideas:

✦ Recycle plastics.

✦ Take one less car trip per week by combining rides or skipping a trip that isn't necessary.

✦ Ride a bike or walk to one event that you normally wouldn't.

✦ Turn the heat or air-conditioning down by 1 degree when you aren't in the house.

✦ Write a letter to your congressperson supporting government programs that help the environment.

✦ Learn about what greenhouse gases are, learn where they come from, learn what La Niña and El Niño are.

because the iron in Earth's core is spinning. Other planets like Mars don't have magnetic fields because they don't have a spinning iron core. Our magnetic field is like a funnel, and it makes all of those particles from the Sun flow down toward the North Magnetic Pole and the South Magnetic Pole. Earth's atmosphere is very thin up at high altitudes, but there is still a small amount of oxygen and nitrogen even up at 50 or 100 or more km (about 30 to 60 mi) above the ground. When the electrons and protons hit that thin atmosphere, it glows green down low and pink and red up high.

When I was on the ISS, I saw the northern lights in December and January and February, and the southern lights in May and June. I remember one particular night when the Sun was very active. I was in the Cupola alone, floating, as we flew through the middle of the southern lights, and our spaceship was surrounded on all sides by that glowing green aurora. I felt like I was in a science fiction movie!

7

DON'T LOOK DOWN: SPACEWALKING

One of the most amazing things you can do in space is leave the comfort and relative safety of your spacefaring vessel to go outside into the unforgiving void of space. To put on the big, bulky spacesuit, open the hatch, and crawl outside. The environment outside of the spaceship is very harsh, and people couldn't survive there for more than a few seconds without a spacesuit.

The American spacesuit that is used for spacewalks is called the EMU, which stands for Extravehicular Mobility Unit. The EMU is essentially like a traveling habitat that an astronaut wears. It has everything necessary to keep an astronaut alive in space, including temperature and pressure regulation and oxygen. Where the ACES suit astronauts wore in the space shuttle can save an

astronaut's life in an emergency situation, the EMU is designed to support life in the harshest environment known to humankind: space.

The EMU is very large and bulky and has a lot of different pieces and parts. It is basically the world's smallest human spaceship, weighing just 125 kg (275 lb). It also has fourteen layers of fabric. The outer layer is very tough so that it doesn't rip or tear—it can even protect us from very small pieces of debris that are zooming around in space at thousands of kilometers per hour. It also helps keep the suit from getting too hot or too cold. There are several layers under this that serve the same function. There is a rubber layer that keeps oxygen inside the suit and prevents leaks. Astronauts wear thin cotton long underwear as a base layer, but on top of that we wear a special, heavy type of long underwear that has plastic tubes sewn into it; those tubes carry cool water to keep our bodies from getting too hot.

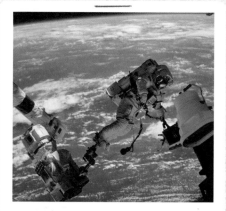

Astronaut on spacewalk in EMU.

PARTS OF THE EMU (EXTRAVEHICULAR MOBILITY UNIT)

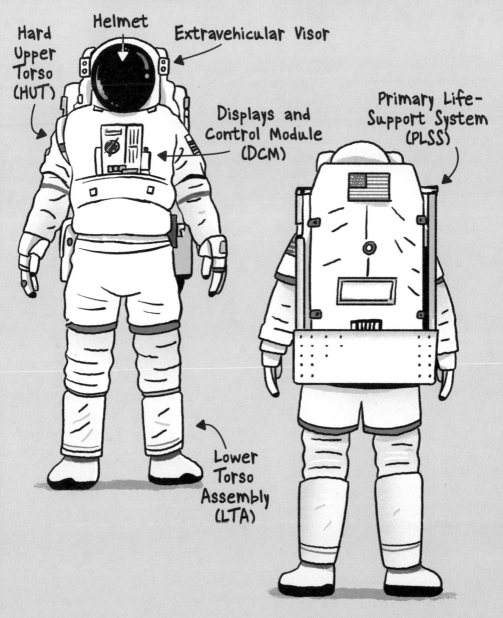

Hard Upper Torso (HUT)

Helmet

Extravehicular Visor

Displays and Control Module (DCM)

Primary Life-Support System (PLSS)

Lower Torso Assembly (LTA)

GETTING DRESSED

It took me several hours to get into the EMU. I put on a heart monitor so mission control could keep an eye on my health, a diaper because I'd be in the suit for eight or nine hours, and long underwear. Then I put on an oxygen mask that is attached to a very long hose to start breathing pure oxygen. This helps your body get rid of nitrogen, which is the biggest part of the air that we normally breathe. But when we go to a lower pressure that nitrogen could come out of our blood and cause serious medical problems, so we breathe pure oxygen for several hours before going into space to clean out as much nitrogen as possible.

About an hour later, I began to get into the actual spacesuit. First I put on the pants, called the LTA (Lower Torso Assembly), which goes from your waist to your knees. That was hard to do in weightlessness because I had to pull hard to push my legs down into them. Next I put on the boots. And then I stuffed myself up into the top half of the spacesuit, called the HUT (Hard Upper Torso), which goes from your stomach to your shoulders. These pieces all attach to one another with metal rings that are airtight.

That can be a problem for our bodies because the suit isn't very flexible and is hard to move around in. After that struggle, all that was left was to put on my helmet and gloves.

I have a giant head, so I had to do a special procedure to put the helmet on. First I rotated the helmet 90 degrees so the front part was over my ears, then I lowered it over my head, then I rotated it back so the front was facing forward. The helmet has lights and cameras on top, and mission control follows each spacewalk by watching the view from these cameras.

The gloves were also a tight fit for me. During the many hours of a spacewalk, I moved around and did all of my work with my hands, so properly fitting gloves were very important. I always had sore forearm and hand muscles after every spacewalk. I also had to wear a giant backpack that has the cooling system, radio, oxygen tanks, and carbon dioxide removal equipment. Plus, there is a cool jet pack that attaches to the backpack that you could use to fly back to the ISS in case you ever accidentally floated away.

Can you hear or feel anything in space?

In outer space there is no air, so sound can't travel from one person to another during a spacewalk. We use radios to talk to each other and to mission control in Houston.

Our spacesuits have systems to keep us from getting too hot or cold, but before I went outside on my spacewalks I was warned by the engineers in Houston that there would be one moment when I would feel cold and another when I would feel hot. And they were right. I was in the front of the ISS working on a dark area. Then, the Sun was shining right on me. I started feeling very strange, like I was being pricked by needles. I knew it was heat but it felt different than normal, like standing next to a fire when you feel heat directly from the flames. It was exactly when and where the engineers had warned me. Another time, I was working in Earth's shadow. Just like the engineers warned me, I started to feel cold, especially my fingertips. The instant the Sun rose, the cold immediately went away. The Sun is a powerful heater!

There are several ways to carry tools and equipment during a spacewalk, and they are very important because there is a lot of work to do. The first place we carry tools is on our chest, on something called a Mini Work Station (MWS). The MWS is a small metal cage that has a lot of places to put tethers, a trash bag, a camera, and tools. Tethers are either cloth or metal strings that can be attached to equipment or hold an astronaut in place while they work. They are some of our most important pieces of equipment because they prevent things (or astronauts) from floating away. And in the weightlessness of space, everything constantly wants to float away.

There is also a control panel on the chest that controls cooling, airflow, and the radio. There is a BRT (Body Restraint Tether) on our left hip that is like a flexible metal hose about 1 m (3 ft) long. It has a clamp on the end that can attach to a piece of the ISS or to a large piece of equipment. After it is attached, you bend the tube to the place you want it, rotate a knob, and it becomes stiff. This can hold astronauts in place while they work, or it can hold a big piece of equipment in place, usually behind us, while we move it from one place on the station to another.

On the right side is a metal piece called a swingarm, where we normally keep a power drill called a PGT (pistol grip tool). It can rotate out in front of you so you can grab it, then when you are finished you put the drill back on the swingarm and rotate it back behind you, out of the way.

Astronaut Sunita L. Williams uses the PGT power drill on a spacewalk on the ISS.

What happens if something goes wrong with your partner?

This happened in 2013 when Italian astronaut Luca Parmitano had a water leak in his spacesuit and it started to fill his helmet with water. He couldn't talk on the radio and he also couldn't see. The other astronaut who was outside with him had to help guide him back to the airlock so he could go back inside the ISS. It was a very dangerous and scary situation! (Not to worry, though, Luca is OK and returned to the ISS for another mission following this incident.)

Astronauts practice for situations like this during spacewalk training runs in the NBL pool, just in case.

PREPARING TO SPACEWALK

One of the biggest jobs before going outside on a spacewalk is getting all of these tools and pieces of equipment ready and organized. Once you are outside, you don't want to waste time looking for something or trying to put tools and equipment in their place. Two bags that we use to organize things are Crew Lock Bags (CLB), which are the size of a small backpack, and Orbital Replacement Units (ORU) bags, which are the size of a large suitcase. We can put all kinds of tools and equipment in them, attach them to the BRT on the spacesuit, and carry them out to the work site. There are hundreds of other unique tools and pieces of equipment that astronauts sometimes use, but these are the basics that we use on every spacewalk.

By the time you put a human into that big spacesuit and add all of that equipment, it can weigh 400 kg (about 880 lb) or more! Plus it is very bulky, so doing simple things like moving in a crowded place or getting into and out of the airlock can be tricky and even painful.

The most important person during this process was another astronaut who stayed inside, called the IV (Intra Vehicular), who helped us get in and out of the spacesuit. It is a very difficult job, and if the IV makes a mistake putting the spacesuit on, it could be very dangerous for the astronauts when they are outside.

ASTRONAUT ACTIVITY

To see how important a tight seal on the airlock hatch is in space, you can practice with a water bottle. Take a standard bottle—a reusable one or a disposable plastic one. Put just a little water into the bottle—no more than half. Put the cap back onto the bottle, and be sure it's locked into place. Then turn the bottle upside down. You want the cap to be on tight, so no water leaks out. In the same way, our hatches need to be tightly pressed against those rubber seals to make sure nothing can leak out.

Why doesn't all the air leak outside when you open the hatch?

During a spacewalk, astronauts go into and out of the ISS through an airlock. It is a module that is divided into two parts: the equipment lock that is attached to the main part of the ISS and the crew lock that leads out to space. The airlock has several very important hatches. There is one between the equipment lock and the Node 1 module in the center of the ISS. There is also a hatch in the middle of the airlock between the crew lock and equipment lock. And there is the main hatch that leads from the crew lock out to space. When a hatch is closed, it presses against rubber seals that keep air from leaking out.

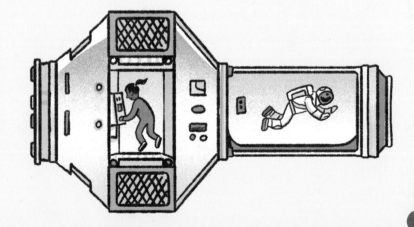

After putting on their spacesuits to get ready for a spacewalk, two astronauts float from the equipment lock into the much smaller crew lock, and an astronaut who is staying inside the ISS closes and seals the hatch behind them.

Next, a pump pulls the air out of the crew lock. When there is very little air left in the crew lock, they open a valve that lets the remaining air out to create a vacuum in the crew lock, which means there is no air. One of the spacewalkers in the crew lock then opens the final hatch that leads them out into space.

When it is time to come back inside, we do everything in reverse. Once the crew lock is filled to the same air pressure as the ISS, the astronaut on the inside opens up the hatch to the equipment lock and pulls the two spacewalkers back inside.

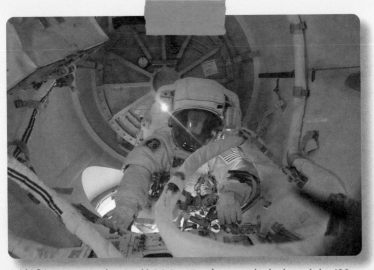

NASA astronaut Jessica U. Meir exits the crew lock aboard the ISS.

RE-ENTRY

BACK TO EARTH

Many people think that launching on a rocket and getting onto orbit is the hardest and most dangerous part of a space mission, but in some ways, coming back to Earth (called "re-entry") is even more difficult. A spaceship has to withstand incredible heat as it re-enters Earth's atmosphere, it has to fly very precisely to get to the right landing site, and its internal life-support systems have to keep the crew inside alive.

My first flight was on the space shuttle *Endeavour*, which is about the size of a big airliner. When we were coming back to Earth, we hit the atmosphere over the Pacific Ocean in the afternoon, but it quickly became nighttime and it was pitch-black outside. We started to feel g-forces from the very thin upper atmosphere pushing on the shuttle. At first, it was only a little bit of force, making us feel like we weighed 10 kg (22 lb). But even that was a lot more than the weightlessness we had felt for the past two weeks. As we held our checklists and pencils, they suddenly started to fall. The force slowly got stronger and stronger until it was almost 2 g's, which means we felt

Endeavour glides to a landing.

twice as heavy as being on Earth. It was like having my best friend sit on top of me while I tried to pilot the space shuttle, while being very dizzy after two weeks of floating.

The air outside our shuttle began to glow— at first pink, then orange, red, and eventually gray. It was an amazing display of glowing fire right outside my pilot's window. There were also bright flashing white lights right above the cockpit. It looked like a strobe light was flashing inside the cockpit as we flew over Central America in the dark of night.

The colors were created by the thin atmosphere around our shuttle turning into plasma, which is an extremely hot form of air. In fact, plasma is so hot that it's not even a gas anymore. You know that the forms of matter are solids, liquids, and gases, but plasma is matter that's superheated, and it's actually its own kind of matter. During re-entry, the temperature got up to 1500°C (2700°F) on the shuttle's nose and wings. After ten minutes of flying through that glowing plasma, it died down and I had a normal nighttime view out of the window. Eventually the g-level came back to 1 g, which is what we all feel down here on Earth.

Five years later, I came back to Earth in a Russian Soyuz capsule, which was a very similar experience to re-entering the atmosphere in the space shuttle (though the landing was quite different). There was a fiery glow outside our window from plasma, and we all felt the g-forces build up. One big difference was that in the Soyuz we got up to 4 g's, so I felt like I weighed four times as much as I do on Earth. That was tough after 200 days of weightlessness. Also, the Soyuz used several different parachutes to slow down, and when the first one deployed, the capsule started tumbling. It felt like I was riding in a bowling ball!

During re-entry, the Soyuz banked to the left and to the right just like the shuttle did, to turn toward our landing site. During one of those bank maneuvers, we had descended from 400 km (about 250 mi) all the way down to about 50 km (about 30 mi), flying over East Africa. As we flew over the Arabian Peninsula, I couldn't believe how fast the ground below was moving. Seeing the ground zooming by at such a low altitude made me realize just how fast spaceships fly.

THE AFTERMATH

There are two words to describe how I felt after both of my space missions: heavy and dizzy. After landing the space shuttle, I had to turn off the power to all of the equipment because I was the pilot, which meant I was the last one to get out of *Endeavour*. I had taken my helmet off while I was turning the computers off, and, when someone came to help get me out of the shuttle, I grabbed my helmet to give it to them. It felt so heavy that I said, "Be careful, this thing weighs 500 pounds!" It didn't really, but I was so used to everything being weightless that even a helmet felt really heavy. A few hours later, I was finally back in my room in the Astronaut Crew Quarters. I got into bed and pulled the covers over me, and it felt like they were made out of lead.

Five years later, after my 200-day mission, I landed in Kazakhstan in the middle of the tundra, which is like a desert with small grass and bushes. After they pulled

Is it better to land in the shuttle or a capsule?

Because the space shuttle used wings and capsules use parachutes, landing in each one is a very different experience. As a pilot, I loved landing in the space shuttle *Endeavour* because I could fly it.

Landing in a capsule was very different. The old Mercury, Gemini, and Apollo capsules all landed in the ocean. The new SpaceX Dragon capsule also lands in the ocean. The Russian Soyuz capsule lands on the ground in Kazakhstan, and Boeing's new Starliner capsule will also land on the ground in the American desert. Personally, I'd rather land on dry ground, because after being in weightlessness, astronauts will not want to be bobbing up and down in ocean waves. But the most important thing is that the capsule is safe.

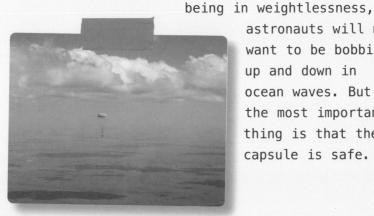
Minutes before landing in the Soyuz capsule.

us out of the Soyuz capsule, they put us in chairs to rest. When I tried to move my head, I felt like I was spinning. That was the most dizzy I have ever felt in my life. NASA had me do several tests to see how my balance was. I had to walk in a straight line, putting one foot right in front of the other, with my eyes closed. That is hard to do on a normal day on Earth. But it is especially tough after 200 days in space! I also had to lie on my stomach and then stand up as quickly as I could. This was to test to see if I got lightheaded. It is what sometimes happens

Terry returns to Earth after 200 days in space!

when you lie on the couch for a while and then suddenly stand up and feel a little dizzy. Some astronauts have that problem after coming back to Earth. Doctors think this is because our bodies lose a lot of fluids while in space and we are dehydrated when we get back to Earth, so astronauts drink a lot of fluids—especially salty ones like sports drinks and even chicken broth—about an hour before landing.

My first few hours back on Earth that second time were really painful because I felt so dizzy. I could walk around and do everything I had to do, but I always wanted someone next to me or to have a handrail to hold. It took twenty-four hours, a helicopter ride, and three passenger jet flights to get from our landing spot in Kazakhstan all the way back to Houston. As soon as I landed in Houston I went straight to the gym, where my specialists helped me start to do rehab. Some of the exercises they made me do were designed to help me improve my balance. I had to walk around or over cones, while swinging a heavy ball over my head. I had to stand on things that were very wobbly to force my balance system to work hard, all while throwing that same heavy ball at a target.

A week after landing, I did a test that measured my body's balance. The scientists and doctors were all shocked—my balance score was better than it had been before I launched, seven months earlier. Even I was surprised. I guess I am lucky because my body was made for spaceflight. But I also think that all of the exercises I did while in space and after I got back to Earth were very important to help me get my balance and my strength back.

Did you meet the president after a space flight?

After both of my spaceflights, I had a chance to go to Washington, DC. NASA sends astronauts to meet with politicians, so they can understand the importance of what we are doing in space. The president decides what kinds of space missions we will do in the future, and Congress decides how much money NASA will get. Without their support, we wouldn't have much of a space program. After my first flight, our crew met with President Obama in the Oval Office. He was very nice and excited to meet us because he loves space.

After both flights, I also went to the House of Representatives and the Senate and talked to about twenty different members of Congress. Some astronauts don't like doing these visits, but I did because I am interested in how our government works.

THE NEXT
MISSION

RETURNING TO THE MOON

It has been more than fifty years since astronauts went to the Moon, and NASA and other space agencies are working very hard to send people back. Artemis is the name of the next NASA program that will send people to the Moon. In Greek mythology, Artemis was Apollo's sister, which is a good name, because this time the American astronauts going to the Moon will be men *and* women. Artemis will have some of the same things that Apollo did: a very large rocket, a capsule for the astronauts, and a Moon lander. The new rocket is called SLS (Space Launch System—not a very exciting name!), the new capsule is called Orion (a little better name), and the lander will be called Starship (built by SpaceX).

NASA's Space Launch System (SLS) and the Orion capsule rollout as part of the Artemis 1 mission.

There will be important differences between Apollo and Artemis. The Apollo missions went directly to the Moon and back to Earth. The longest mission was less than two weeks. Typical Artemis missions will last between one and two months, because they will spend time at a small space station orbiting the Moon called Gateway. Also, Apollo flew eleven missions in four years, but Artemis will only fly one mission per year.

The goal of Apollo was to prove that we could send a person to the Moon and return them safely to Earth, and it did that perfectly. We also learned a lot about our Moon

Concept image of the SpaceX HLS Starship, which could one day take astronauts back to the Moon as part of NASA's Artemis program.

Is there gravity in space?

There is gravity everywhere in the whole universe. You cannot escape it no matter where you go. So when you hear people talk about zero g, or no gravity, in space, that is not technically correct. The ISS orbits about 400 km (250 mi) above the ground, and at that altitude Earth's gravity is almost 90 percent as strong as it is down here on the planet. In fact, all the way at the Moon, there's still a small amount of gravitational pull from Earth. And if you go out to other planets, like Mars, Jupiter, or even to other stars in our galaxy, there is still a very tiny bit of gravitational pull from our planet. The same is true of every other planet, or Moon, or even person. That's right, your body makes a little bit of gravity and you pull on every other thing in the universe! Now, it's not very much, and you could never measure it, but that kind of makes you feel important, doesn't it?

and solar system. But the goal of Artemis will be to make a more permanent home on and near the Moon, with the hope of eventually sending people to Mars.

THE TRIP TO MARS

Going to Mars will be much harder than going to the Moon. The big difference is the distance. The Moon is about 380,000 km (238,000 mi) from Earth, but Mars is much farther away. Depending on where Earth and Mars are as they orbit the Sun, it can be as close as 55,000,000 km (more than 34,000,000 mi) or as far away as 400,000,000 km (nearly 250,000,000 mi). In fact, when Mars is on the other side of the Sun from Earth, at its farthest point, it takes light or radio waves more than twenty minutes to make a one-way trip. So if you were on Earth and trying to have a conversation with an astronaut on Mars, you would each have to wait forty minutes for a reply every time you said something. That would be awkward.

Sun   Earth   Mars

A trip to the Moon takes about three days. But missions to Mars using normal rockets would take more than six months. Then astronauts would have to wait a year and a half for the two planets to go around the Sun before they could leave Mars to return to Earth, so the total round trip to Mars and back would take about three years.

Besides making the trip quicker, there are other things that we need to work on. One of the most important is to make equipment more reliable so it doesn't break down often. This equipment includes machines that provide oxygen to breathe and water to drink and take carbon dioxide out of the atmosphere. We call these jobs life support, and without them astronauts would die within days. Although the ISS has special equipment for these tasks, those machines break down often and require a lot of time and spare parts to repair them. We will also need a lot of electrical power to run this equipment, and because we will be so far from the Sun, solar panels won't provide enough electricity on their own. We will need nuclear reactors to make the required electricity for the machines, particularly during the night on Mars, which is about as long as night on Earth is. Solar power won't work on the Moon because there would be no power during the two-week-long night.

We will also need a lander—a special spaceship that can take us from orbit down to the planet's surface. A Moon lander is a little bit simpler than a Mars lander because there is no atmosphere on the Moon and its gravity is pretty weak, about one-sixth of Earth's gravity. Mars is more difficult because it is a bigger planet, with three-eighths of Earth's gravity. It also has a thin atmosphere, so a lander will need a special heat shield to survive all of the heat and friction it will face when it flies through Mars' atmosphere as it is slowing down to land.

After the astronauts land, they will need special spacesuits for walking on the surface. The Moon and Mars both have a lot of dust, so those spacesuits will need to have a tough outer layer so they don't get damaged by dust particles. Their spacesuits will also have to be lighter and easier to move around in than the spacesuits I used on the ISS, where I was weightless. On the surface of Mars there is a decent amount of gravity, and a suit as bulky as the EMU would be too heavy to move around in.

Moon lander.

Are there aliens?

I have never seen aliens. I haven't
even see anything strange or unexplained,
like a UFO. That doesn't mean that they aren't
out there. But we have a few big problems in
trying to find them.

The first is distance.
We've sent robotic probes
or rovers to all of the
planets in our solar
system, and there is
no obvious life on
any of them. If there
is advanced life out
there in the universe,
it would be on planets orbiting other stars.
NASA has launched several space telescopes, like
Kepler, Spitzer, TESS, and others, to look for
such planets. They've shown us that there are
probably billions of planets in the universe,
some of them very similar to Earth.

Another problem is
communicating with other
civilizations. Radio
signals from Earth are
too weak to travel great
distances, and the noise
from our Sun would drown
these signals.

Kepler space telescope.

SOARING THROUGH SPACE

If you add up all of the times I circled Earth on my two spaceflights, I traveled about 141 million km (nearly 88 million mi). The space station flies at about 27,600 kmh (more than 17,000 mph), there are twenty-four hours in a day, and I was in space for a total of 213.5 days. If you multiply all of those together, you get a very big number—141,422,400 km (87,875,800 mi).

The ISS flies around Earth about sixteen times per day, which means I did more than 3,400 orbits of our planet during my seven months in space. One trip around Earth is more than 40,000 km (about 25,000 mi), so it was a lot of traveling around the planet. This only includes the distance I traveled over the surface of Earth. While I was on orbit, our planet was also going around the Sun, at about 107,000 kmh (about 66,000 mph). That is even faster than our spaceships orbiting Earth! I have been traveling that fast around our Sun ever since I was born, and so have you, so that is a lot of kilometers traveled around our solar system. If you do the math, it comes out to 50 billion km (31 billion mi) that I have traveled around the Sun during my lifetime.

But it doesn't stop there. Our Sun is flying around our Milky Way galaxy at 720,000 kmh (more than 447,000 mph), with respect to the black hole at the center of our galaxy. So we are moving even *faster* through the galaxy. And as you can imagine, our galaxy is moving around other galaxies even faster than that. So, everything in the universe is moving constantly, and when you ask how far you've traveled, you really need to ask how far did you travel over the surface of Earth or around the solar system or around our galaxy. It's fun to think about how big and amazing the universe is.

Can you time travel?

Ask an Astronaut

You can—and I did—time travel in space! Well, sort of. A scientist named Albert Einstein came up with the theory of relativity more than one hundred years ago. Einstein's theory stated that if you are traveling very fast (special relativity) or if you are accelerating very quickly (general relativity), time will actually slow down for you, relative to someone else.

Imagine you and your friends set your watches to the same time. If one friend flies close to the speed of light and then comes back, their watch will be slower than yours! Yours might say 11 a.m. and theirs would show 10 a.m. Both watches are correct—less time actually passed for them.

NASA scientists told me after my last spaceflight that I was seven milliseconds younger than I would have been if I hadn't flown in space. So, in a way, I time traveled. The fancy term for this is called time dilation, and when comparing a person at rest and a person accelerating very quickly, the person at rest and the person flying around very fast both FEEL as though time is passing normally. The astronaut will look at their watch and it will be clicking at a normal rate. It's only when they look at their friend's watch that they will see a difference in time.

MEASURING THE UNIVERSE

Other stars and galaxies and planets are really, *really* far from Earth, and it is difficult to use normal units of distance when you talk about them. When it comes to planets and our solar system, we came up with a unit of measurement called the AU (Astronomical Unit). One AU is 150,000,000 km (more than 93,000,000 mi). It's the distance from Earth to the Sun. In other words, Earth is 1 AU from the Sun. So we can either say that Neptune is 4,500,000,000 km (about 2,800,000,000 mi) from the Sun, or we can say that it orbits 30 AU from the Sun, or 30 times as far as Earth does.

Our galaxy, the Milky Way, is 1,000,000,000,000,000,000 km (more than 621,000,000,000,000,000 mi) across. One quintillion km. That is a lot of zeros. As you measure the distance to other galaxies across the universe, there are even more zeros.

Because light moves very fast, traveling about 300,000 km (about 186,000 mi) in one second, we

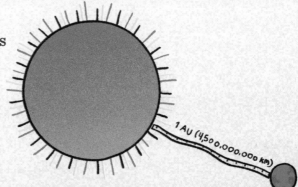

1 AU (4,500,000,000 km)

sometimes measure extreme distance in light-years. A light-year is simply the distance that light can travel in one year. It's about 9,500,000,000,000 km (nearly 6,000,000,000,000 mi). A light-year is not only a measure of distance, but also of time. When you see light from a star or galaxy, you know how far away it is, but also how old that light is.

So how far away are things in terms of light-years? Our nearest star, Proxima Centauri, is 4.22 light-years away. It would take you 4.22 years to travel there if you were traveling at the speed of light. Most stars that you can see with your eyes are between 10 and 1,000 light-years away. The nearest galaxy to us, the Andromeda Galaxy, is 2.5 million light-years away. And some of the farthest galaxies that the Hubble Space telescope has seen are 12 billion light-years away!

YOUR TRAINING
BEGINS HERE

My dream of being an astronaut began when I was in kindergarten, when I read my first book. It was about the Apollo missions to the Moon, and I was hooked. I grew up with posters of airplanes and rockets on the walls of my room as a boy. I eventually learned about the things I would have to do in order to become an astronaut, and I made a plan.

I went to the Air Force Academy, flew F-16 fighter jets, and eventually became a test pilot. I also majored in applied mathematics at the Academy and minored in French. I did an exchange with a family in Finland, spent a semester in college in France, and did several assignments flying F-16s overseas. That international experience was very important to NASA, because we have an *International* Space Station, and astronauts have to be able to work with people from many different countries.

Three-year-old Terry flying in a small propeller plane.

All of these experiences were important for me because they allowed me to position myself as a strong candidate when NASA decided to hire a new astronaut class. It definitely wasn't guaranteed that I would be selected—thousands of very smart and talented people were also applying for just a few astronaut slots. But I knew I had given myself my best shot because of the work I did.

My work and preparation taught me an important lesson that is good for kids and adults: Don't tell yourself no!

When I was a kid, if I had told myself it was too difficult to become an astronaut, and that I had no chance, I never would have put in the work and, ultimately, gotten selected. But I knew that becoming an astronaut was something I wanted to try for, and I had some ability in math and science and flying, so I went for it. I did the hard work of getting a math degree and studying in France and learning to fly jets. I did have some luck when NASA selected me, but I have found that the harder you work, the luckier you get! So, no matter what your dream is, I have one very important piece of advice:

Don't tell yourself no.

That applies to just about anything you want to do in life. Some kids want to grow up to be astronauts, and that is great. This book can help give you a good starting line. But some might want to be scientists—studying how the universe works—or how to make new materials or how to cure diseases or any one of a million interesting subjects. Some might want to be engineers—learning how to build new airplanes or cars—or how to make medical devices work better or how to build just about anything you can dream up. Some kids might want to grow up to run a company or to be a doctor or a pilot. There are so many fun and cool jobs that you can have when you grow up!

For me, space is what ignited the most interest and excitement. The universe is infinite, there is so much to learn, and the idea of floating and looking back at our beautiful planet was a huge motivator for me. For you

there may be something else that really interests you. No matter what that is, education is really important. I am still learning, even to this day! So be sure you focus on your education.

Exploring the infinite universe.

Perhaps most importantly, be curious about the world (and the universe) around you. Always ask questions and be excited to learn new things. If you focus on education and stay curious your whole life, you will be successful at anything you try!

If you want to be an astronaut, you need to go for it. You have been given unique gifts and talents and abilities, and you are special. You're unlike any other kid in the world! Even though the dream of becoming an astronaut may seem daunting, even if no one in your family has done anything like it, and even if none of your friends think you can do it, remember that *one thing* makes any wild dream possible: Your belief in yourself. The journey to pursuing your dreams begins with *you*. Before the hard work, the training, the emergency simulations, and the spacewalks in the pool, you have to believe you're capable, and then put in the work.

And remember once more: Don't tell yourself no on the way to achieving your dreams. There may be plenty of obstacles, but never let yourself be one of them!

A GUIDE TO ASTRONAUT TERMS

Airlock: A module where astronauts get dressed in their spacesuits to do spacewalks. It uses a series of hatches to allow them to go outside in the vacuum of space while keeping air pressure inside the ISS.

CAPCOM (pronounced "cap comm"): Capsule Communicator; the person in mission control who talks on the radio to the astronauts in space.

Capsule: A small spacecraft that uses parachutes to land when it comes back to Earth.

CATO ("kay toe"): Communications and tracking officer; the flight controller in MCC responsible for radios, antennae, and other communications gear.

ECLSS ("eee kliss"): Environmental and Life Support System; the flight controller in MCC responsible for the spacecraft's air and water for the crew.

EMU: Extravehicular Mobility Unit; The big white spacesuit that astronauts use to do spacewalks on the ISS.

EVA ("eva"): Extravehicular Activity; the flight controller responsible for spacewalks.

FDO ("fie dough"): Flight dynamics officer; the flight controller responsible for the vehicle's trajectory during launch and landing, and making sure it stays on course.

FLIGHT: Flight director, the person in mission control responsible for the mission's success.

ISO ("eye so"): Inventory and storage officer; the flight controller responsible for keeping track of where all of the equipment is stored.

ISS: International Space Station; a cooperative effort between international space agencies to establish a permanent orbiting base of scientific operations in space.

MCC: Mission Control Center; the building on Earth where flight controllers and engineers control space missions.

ODIN ("oh-din"): Onboard Data Interfaces and Network; the flight controller responsible for making sure the computers work.

OPSPLAN ("ops plan"): Operations planner; the flight controller responsible for managing the crew's work schedule.

Orbiter: The part of the space shuttle system that looked like an airplane, and used wings to land on a runway when it came back to Earth.

PHALCON ("falcon"): Power, Heating, Articulation, Lighting Control; the flight controller responsible for the electrical power on the ISS.

ROBO ("row bow"): Robotics; the flight controller responsible for the various robotic arms on the vehicle.

THOR ("thor"): Thermal Operations and Resources; the flight controller responsible for keeping the ISS from getting too hot or too cold.

INDEX

TERRY VIRTS

Colonel (USAF retired) Terry Virts has spent more than seven months in space during his two spaceflights, piloting the space shuttle *Endeavour* on STS-130 in 2010 and commanding the International Space Station during Expedition 42/43 in 2014 and 2015. He served in the US Air Force as a fighter pilot, test pilot, and NASA astronaut and is a graduate of the US Air Force Academy, Embry-Riddle Aeronautical University, and Harvard Business School. He is currently working in the energy industry to help focus on renewable, green energy technologies.

Virts hosts the *Down to Earth with Terry Virts* podcast and is the author of *How to Astronaut: Everything You Need to Know Before Leaving Earth*, as well as the National Geographic photography book *View From Above*. He also directed the documentary *One More Orbit* and helped shoot the IMAX film *A Beautiful Planet* from the ISS.